THE
MANY FACES
OF
WORLD WAR I

by Irving Werstein

JULIAN MESSNER, INC.
NEW YORK

Published by Julian Messner, Inc.
8 West 40th Street, New York 18

Published simultaneously in Canada
by The Copp Clark Publishing Co. Limited

© Copyright 1963 by Irving Werstein

Printed in the United States of America
Library of Congress Catalog Card No. 63–16800

This book is dedicated to the memory of my friend, Lou Sorin, actor, gentleman and teller of tales, who was a doughboy in France during the First World War.

ACKNOWLEDGMENTS

I wish to thank the staff of the American History Room in The New York Public Library for assisting me during the preparation of *The Many Faces of World War I*. I was given gracious help at The New York Historical Society, as well. The Historical Division, Department of the Army, supplied much valuable data.

Many veterans of World War I provided me with personal reminiscences; I am most grateful to the late Lou Sorin whose vivid tales of actions in the Argonne Forest brought that grim warfare to stark reality.

In recreating an era of history, I have always found the newspapers of the day an invaluable source of colorful information; the courteous staff of The New York Public Library Newspaper Collection was always ready to serve.

Again I must especially thank my editors, Miss Gertrude Blumenthal and Miss Lee Hoffman; if this work has merit, they must share the credit for their keen and specific criticisms of earlier drafts.

My agent Miss Candida Donadio provided both morale and advice; my wife and young son were patient and understanding. I would be remiss if I did not have a special word of gratitude for Mrs. Lee Levin who typed the manuscript.

New York   I.W.
May, 1963

CONTENTS

PART ONE

1914—Blighted War

PART TWO

1915-1916—The Battering Ram

PART THREE

1917-1918—The Last Full Measure

I have a rendezvous with Death
At some disputed barricade,
When Spring comes back with rustling shade
And apple-blossoms fill the air—
I have a rendezvous with Death
When Spring brings back blue days and fair.

ALAN SEEGER, killed in action, 1916, on a battlefield of France while serving as an American volunteer with the French Foreign Legion

PART ONE

« 1914 »
BLIGHTED YEAR

The lamps are going out all over Europe;
we shall not see them lit again in our
lifetime.
SIR EDWARD GREY, Viscount of Falldon—
August, 1914

Europe, 1914

1

A SUNDAY IN JUNE

THE ARCHDUKE FRANZ FERDINAND, HEIR PRESUMPTIVE TO THE throne of the Austro-Hungarian Empire, was in a jovial mood on Sunday, June 28, 1914. The Austrian army maneuvers he had attended for nearly two weeks were ended. This year the exercises had been run in the fields and mountains of Bosnia, a territory annexed by Austria in 1908 from the kingdom of Serbia.

The maneuvers had gone well, and Franz Ferdinand was highly pleased by the performance of his troops. But it was not that alone which made him happy. He had a more personal reason. This day his beloved wife, Sophie, Duchess of Hohenberg, had motored down from Vienna to join him in Sarajevo, the Bosnian capital.

The Archduke, eldest nephew of aged Emperor Franz Josef, who had ruled the empire since 1848, was a haughty man with few friends. Franz Ferdinand was particularly disliked in Bosnia, where the population, mostly Slavs of Serbian descent, hungered for reunification with their mother country, Serbia.

To the Bosnians, he epitomized Austrian tyranny. His reception by villagers, peasants and townspeople during the maneuvers had been distinctly hostile. But the Archduke ignored the cool treatment. This last Sunday in June, he vowed, was going to be a pleasant day.

Despite the sentiments of the city's residents, ancient Sarajevo had been bedecked and beflagged in the Austrian colors to honor the royal visitors. The Archduke and the Duchess were to attend a ceremony at the Town Hall and then drive to the palace on the outskirts. After remaining a few additional days in Bosnia, they would return to Vienna.

Advisers tried to dissuade Franz Ferdinand from traveling through Sarajevo in an open touring car. Security officers feared an attempt on his life by Serbian nationalists. But the Archduke was stubborn as well as haughty and refused to consider riding in an enclosed vehicle.

"No one here has reason to harm me. I will not hide from my people. I am the best friend the Bosnians have," the Archduke said.

It was paradoxical that Franz Ferdinand should have enemies in Sarajevo. Of all the Austro-Hungarian ruling clique, he alone advocated full rights and equality for the Bosnians. Only recently he had proposed that the empire be broadened to include as a full member, not merely Bosnia, but also those southern Slav provinces owned by Austria's partner, Hungary. According to him, these regions should be formed into a separate state of the empire on a par with Austria and Hungary.

Instead of ensuring his popularity, this advanced concept bred enmity against him at home, in Hungary and among the Serbs. Conservative Austrians were outraged that the successor to the throne even suggested equality for such "inferiors" as Bosnians and Slavs. The idea of surrendering territory— even troublesome areas that constantly seethed with insurrection—irritated the Hungarians. To Serbian nationalists, Franz Ferdinand's moderation was hated more than the present tyranny. One day, the Archduke would wear the crown and have the power to create a new Slavic state. When that time came, the dream of a Serbia united with her lost provinces would be forever doomed.

For all these reasons, not even the sunny June weather brought smiles to the crowds lining the route of the Archduke's motorcade. Cavalrymen in gay uniforms trotted on both sides of the large touring car bearing Franz Ferdinand and Sophie. The streets were guarded by soldiers and police. The military governor of Bosnia, General Potiorek, had organized ample protection for the couple.

The automobiles wended slowly to the Town Hall along beflagged Appel Quay, which paralleled the Milliâca River. Antagonistic faces and cold eyes greeted the procession. No sound came from the spectators; the clomping hooves of the cavalry horses echoed loudly on the cobblestones.

Nevertheless, the Archduke smiled and waved at the mute crowd, while the Duchess bowed her head left and right. They were rewarded by a deep, sullen silence. As the cars rolled across a bridge there was sudden movement among the spectators; a black object arched through the air. It hit the open hood of the touring car and bounced onto the pavement.

"A bomb!" somebody gasped.

There was a jarring explosion. Pieces of jagged metal slammed against the rear of the automobile. A cavalryman toppled to the pavement, his gaudy uniform stained with blood. A woman onlooker screamed and fell writhing to the cobblestones.

Amid excited shouting, policemen with drawn sabers charged the crowd. The motorcade picked up speed. Moments later the cars stopped at the Town Hall, where the burgomaster, unaware of the occurrence a few blocks away, hurried down the steps to greet the visitors.

Franz Ferdinand stood up in the tonneau of his car. His voice shook as he shouted at the burgomaster, "Is this how you prove your loyalty to the crown? With bombs?"

The flustered burgomaster stammered an apology. The culprits would be caught and punished, he promised. What had happened was a crime, a blot on Sarajevo, on Bosnia, on every loyal subject of the Emperor.

At last Franz Ferdinand calmed down sufficiently to go on with the program, which was somewhat dampened by the bombing incident. There was a speech by the burgomaster; a chorus of schoolchildren sang; and a little girl presented a bouquet to the Duchess.

A few moments before noon the affair ended. No one was in a festive mood as the Archduke ordered the cavalcade to leave. General Potiorek, seeking to ease the situation, made a lame joke.

"I am certain there will be no further attempts against our guests," he said. "Bosnians never try assassination twice in one day." His sally fell flat and nobody laughed. Franz Ferdinand glared at the crestfallen general and stepped into the waiting car.

With an imperious wave of his hand, he signaled the chauffeur to start. The cavalcade moved out. As it proceeded up Appel Quay no notice was given to a sunken-cheeked eighteen-year-old youth who lurked in the doorway of a barber shop located at the intersection of Rudolf Street and Appel Quay.

When the Archduke's car drew abreast of the barber shop, the youth suddenly bolted past police and cavalry guards and leaped upon the running board of the automobile. Before anyone could grab him, he yanked a Browning automatic from his pocket and fired six shots. The first bullet struck the Duchess low in the right side. The second hit Franz Ferdinand in his throat, piercing the jugular vein. The rest of the fusillade went wild. A horseman struck the killer with his saber. The assassin fell to the pavement and struggled to his feet as a swarm of guards seized him.

In the car, Duchess Sophie slumped back against the leather seat. Eyes glazing as her life ebbed, she turned to the Archduke lying lifeless at her side, blood spurting from his throat and staining his white uniform jacket. With her last strength, she gasped, "Franz, are you dying?"

Then she, too, was dead.

The murderer, a Serbian student named Gavrilo Princip, belonged to a fanatical nationalist society ominously named Union or Death! Its members were sworn to use bullet, bomb or knife against the Austro-Hungarian Empire until Bosnia was reunited with Serbia.

Already ravaged by tuberculosis, Princip survived in prison until 1918. Up to the moment of his death he showed neither remorse nor regret for his desperate act, although it started a four-year-long war which eventually involved thirty nations, including the United States of America.

The conflict, fought in Europe, Asia and Africa, took nearly 20 million lives, cost $338 billion and almost destroyed Western civilization. No count could be made of the millions who were maimed, disfigured, blinded and blighted. No man could estimate the damage wrought by pestilence, plague, disease and famine. The world-wide agony caused by Princip's bullets left hundreds of thousands uprooted and homeless. All this was the aftermath of the First World War. Perhaps the most ghastly result was that it planted the seeds for another, more deadly conflict, a mere generation later.

2

"IT NEEDS ONLY A SPARK . . ."

THE NEWS OF WHAT HAD HAPPENED IN REMOTE SARAJEVO
spread throughout Europe and was flashed by cable to the
United States. Extra editions of newspapers were hawked in
the streets of Rome, Berlin, St. Petersburg, Vienna, Belgrade,
Paris and Budapest.

That warm June night the talk in cafés, bistros, coffee-
houses, restaurants and pubs from the Thames River to the
shores of the Volga River revolved around the double killing
in the old city that stood beside the Milliâca River.

No one could foretell what consequences might result. But
from cabinet minister to peasant, every European realized
that Sunday, June 28, 1914, was a day of destiny. Lights
burned late in the ministries and war offices. By Monday
morning the Continent was agog with rumors. The Austrian
secret service claimed the assassination plot had been hatched
in Belgrade with the complicity of the Serbian government.

However, the next breeze carried another whisper: Franz
Ferdinand's domestic enemies had arranged his murder. Back
and forth flew the rumors. War was imminent. There would
be no war. Revolution had broken out in Bosnia. Emperor
Franz Josef had suffered a heart attack at the news. Moments
of dread and uncertainty were followed by hope and
optimism.

Telephones jangled and telegraph keys clicked with diplomatic messages to the capitals of Europe. Crowds gathered

before governmental offices to await word of new developments. In Vienna, roving mobs cried for vengeance and stoned the Serbian embassy. Despite such manifestations, few Austro-Hungarians actually wanted war against Serbia.

Thinking men realized that Austrian military action might involve all Europe in a terrible conflict. If Austria marched, Russia was pledged to aid Serbia. Germany would then support Austria. England and France were aligned by treaty with Russia. Thus Europe faced widespread hostilities for the first time since Napoleon Bonaparte's armies had scourged the Continent.

Europe had not enjoyed tranquility in the first fourteen years of the twentieth century. The Franco-Prussian War had erupted; Russia lost to Japan in 1904–1905; and several small wars had flared in the Balkans between 1900–1913. No one took Balkan wars seriously. That region had always been in ferment, wtih a dozen nations and a score of nationalities constantly struggling for power.

The big countries—Britain, France, Italy, Germany, Austro-Hungary and Russia—lived in a condition of "tenuous peace." These nations jockeyed for position and advantage. The alignment of forces had long been chosen.

On the one hand was the Triple Alliance (also known as the Central Powers): Germany, Austro-Hungary and Italy; on the other, the Triple Entente: England, France and Russia. European diplomacy was a chess game of wits, skill, loyalties and ambitions. Except for France, the nations in both camps were monarchies. King George V of England was the ruler of a vast empire, the greatest in the world's history. It included India, Australia, wide areas of Africa and remote Pacific Islands. Its expanse was so huge that the sun never set on the British flag, for George's realm girdled the globe and was never totally in darkness.

Kaiser Wilhelm II, of the Hohenzollern family, sat on the

German throne. Perhaps because he had been born with a withered left arm the Kaiser was an overly arrogant individual; perhaps that defect made him strive harder to be the superior of everyone else. A contemporary journalist wrote about the Kaiser: ". . . in Wilhelm we have a man both unstable and unpredictable . . . a man who tailors his principles to suit his whims."

It had only been in 1864 that Germany rose from a jigsaw puzzle of petty states and princedoms to become a powerful nation dominated by Prussian militarism. The creator of the new Germany was Prince Otto von Bismarck, chancellor of Prussia, whom historians call "the ablest statesman of the nineteenth century." Bismarck forged unification of his country by both force of arms and political maneuvering.

In 1890, two years after ascending the throne, Wilhelm II removed Bismarck from office. "The Kaiser could not bear to keep a man of strong will around him," a commentator noted. However, the Germany of 1914 still benefited from Bismarck's achievements. Known as the "Iron Chancellor," Bismarck had raised Germany to its greatest glory by crushing France in the war of 1870–1871.

Until then, the French had been the foremost military and political force in Europe. The defeat by the Germans toppled Emperor Louis Napoleon III from the throne and made France a republic. Bismarck inflicted a peace on France so severe that it left her a second-rate power. By the treaty's terms, the French ceded to Germany the mining regions of Alsace-Lorraine and also paid huge reparations in money.

Although France had been humbled, every Frenchman saw in Alsace-Lorraine a reason for hating the Germans. The loss of those provinces was a blot on French honor, a stain that could not be wiped out until the disgrace of 1870–1871 had been washed away in German blood.

Only one enemy existed for Frenchmen—the Germans,

whom they called *les salles boches,* the dirty butchers. No French child went to bed without offering a prayer for the return of Alsace-Lorraine and the downfall of Germany. To hate *les salles boches* was a natural condition for Frenchmen.

The Germans well knew French sentiment. Back in 1871 as the Franco-Prussian War guns fell silent, Field Marshal Graf Helmuth von Moltke, commanding the triumphant German armies predicted: "What our sword has won in half a year, our sword must guard for half a century."

The Kaiser heeded this admonition. In all the world no nation boasted an army to equal the German *Reichswehr.* Wilhelm's soldiers were equipped with modern arms: magazine-loading Mauser rifles and Maxim machine guns gave them superiority in fire power over any potential enemy. German artillery, manufactured in the giant armament works owned by Alfred Krupp, was among the best in the world. Krupp had secretly turned out heavy artillery of 320 mm. and 240 mm. caliber, bigger than any made before. These mammoth guns were only one of Germany's military surprises—the Kaiser had many more.

However, the most powerful weapon in the German arsenal, according to an American observer, "was an unmatched and unsurpassed efficiency in organization and discipline."

With good reason, Kaiser Wilhelm II feared no country in Europe. The prime enemy, France, had the second best army on the Continent—but second best was not good enough.

France's allies, Russia and England, were militarily far inferior to Germany. Russia's biggest asset was a seemingly endless supply of manpower. In the nineteenth century, this might have been a decisive factor, but numbers alone could not win a modern war. Industrial output, railroads, communication, technical skill, training and equipment were critical in a twentieth century conflict.

The Russian despot, Tsar Nicholas II, of the Romanoff

lineage, was an irresolute man whose court was dominated by self-seeking, inefficient advisers. Most of his generals were corrupt bunglers; the Russian army was filled with incompetent officers who only could lead the brave and faithful Russian common soldier to disaster.

Because he was so weak and indecisive, the Tsar allowed Grigori Rasputin, a self-styled "monk," to dominate much of his thinking. Rasputin held a tremendous influence over the Tsarina Alexandra, and through her, reached the Tsar.

An evil genius, Rasputin posed as a seer who could read the future. After winning the favor of Russia's rulers, he acquired a big following of cabinet ministers, government officials and army bigwigs. Apparently they visited Rasputin for his advice; in fact, they bribed the schemer to mention them to the Tsar for promotion and higher office.

In 1914, Russia belonged to another era in her development. The Russian people were mainly illiterate peasants —"The Dark People," a novelist called them, because ignorance, superstition and ritual ruled their lives. Still a semifeudal land of wealthy aristocrats and poverty-stricken masses, Russia lagged far behind the other European great powers in industrial development. She lacked railroads and highways; communications were poor over the tremendous stretches of Russia.

Misery and discontent boiled throughout the Tsar's domain. Yet millions of his subjects worshipped the "Little Father" who sat upon the throne. They believed he ruled by Divine Right, and he was, to them, a religious as well as temporal figure.

Not all Russians regarded the Tsar with such awed respect. Although industrial workers were few in proportion to peasants, the militant Russian working class, or "proletariat," numbered many thousands. Centered in cities such as St. Petersburg, Moscow and Kiev were mechanics, machinists, metal workers and other laborers. In their ranks were nihilists, anarchists, socialists and communists. These left-wing radicals spread dissatisfaction among the workers and formed the core of a strong revolutionary movement.

In 1905, after the debacle of the Japanese war, the left-wingers brought on a revolution to overthrow the Tsar. The insurrection was bloodily crushed, but not until mutinies had broken out in the Russian Army and Navy. The uprising should have prodded the Tsar to decree social and political reforms on a wide scale. Instead, except for granting a little more power to the *Duma* (Parliament), the Russian ruler tightened his tyrannical grip on the nation.

The secret police, the *Cheka,* rounded up radicals and subversives. After drumhead trials, the left-wingers were marched off to exile in remote regions of Siberia. "There they can propagandize the snow drifts, the ice floes and the timber wolves," sneered a *Cheka* official. Such revolutionaries as Nikolai Lenin, Josef Stalin, Leon Trotsky and others served periods in Siberia but eventually escaped to agitate among the Russian workers.

The Kaiser knew that the Russian armies were huge, but felt that his ally, Austria, could defeat Russia if bolstered by German officers and troops. In the event of a war with France, Wilhelm's generals assured him that there was "no threat from the East."

"Russian railroads are so bad, the roads so poor, the army so inefficient, that it would take weeks to mobilize and move her armies to the frontier. By then, we shall be drinking tea in St. Petersburg," a German staff officer boasted.

The Kaiser regarded England as even less dangerous than Russia. According to him, the British Army was "contemptible." In German military circles, there was a current joke that the Berlin police would "arrest the British Army" if war came.

The Germans made a bad mistake in underestimating the "Old Contemptibles," which the British Army promptly labeled itself when the remark became known. Although small in size, the British Regular Army was splendidly trained, disciplined and equipped. No soldier in the world matched "Tommy Atkins," the ordinary British regular, for courage, stamina, morale, fighting qualities and, above all, a sense of humor.

England for centuries had stressed her Navy and not her Army. The English believed "who ruled the seas, ruled the world." Until 1900 the Royal Navy's command of the oceans had been challenged only by Napoleon. But at the turn of the twentieth century, Germany started a naval construction program intended to outstrip the English fleet.

The Germans widened the Kiel Canal for easier access to the North Sea and began building a big navy. By 1914, the Kaiser's fleet still did not match the British. In the dreadnought class (modern big-gun, high-speed battleships) the Germans lagged by only seven ships—they had thirteen, the British, twenty. For all classes of 1914-style warships—dreadnoughts, pre-dreadnoughts, battle cruisers, armored cruisers and destroyers—the total count was 177 British ships and 87 German.

Although outnumbered nearly two to one in ships, the size of the German Navy did not fully mirror its strength. The Kaiser's naval designers and inventors were hard at work perfecting and improving submarines, torpedoes and new types of mines.

The ever-growing German Navy caused grave concern in England. In 1900, when the Kaiser had announced his intention to build a large fleet, crusty Lord John Fisher, the First Lord of the Admiralty, stated, "The German Navy must be wiped out as we would burn a nest of vipers."

The combined Austro-Hungarian and German navies were far smaller than the French and British fleets, but never in modern times had England's control of the seas been so precarious. The German Navy was mastering an unconventional kind of sea warfare by developing novel tactics for her U-boats (submarines) which would soon make the underwater craft the scourge of the oceans.

Long before Gavrilo Princip shot Franz Ferdinand, Colonel Edward M. House, a special adviser to United States President Woodrow Wilson, wrote from Berlin, "The situation here is extraordinary. It is militarism run stark mad." The colonel was referring to the open ambitions the Kaiser had for his nation. Not only did Wilhelm seek to wrest control of the seas from Britain, but he also meant to have a colonial empire even greater than England's.

"Deutschland über alles!"—Germany above all—ran the opening lines of that nation's anthem. The words expressed the national aspirations, to be the world's supreme power. The Kaiser's plans included building a long-projected German-controlled railway from Berlin to Baghdad and the Persian oil fields.

German domination of the Balkans was a first step toward this goal. But Serbia stood in the way. To remove this stumbling block, the Germans intrigued against the Serbs by concluding secret agreements with Bulgaria and Turkey. The other important Balkan power, Rumania, swayed indecisively, first toward Germany and then from her. But Rumania presented no problems.

"Should the Rumanians stand in our path, we shall step on them," declared a German general.

The Kaiser had other targets. He greedily eyed the farmlands of the Russian Ukraine. There lay all the land he needed for *lebensraum*—living space—in which Germany could expand. And there, too, were the fertile fields which could grow the wheat, the barley, the crops, to feed his visionary Greater Germany.

Thus, in 1914, Europe seethed with suspicion, distrust and plotting from the North Sea to the Caspian Sea. The whole Continent boiled and shook. An era was ending for Europe— for the world. An age was dying without mourners.

No man dared admit the imminence of its death. The last few weeks of the old world with its kings, emperors, tsars, dukes and princes were ticking away. After this fateful summer of 1914, nothing would ever again be the same. But despite the rumblings, people apparently ignored the impending earthquake.

Bands played Viennese waltzes; couples strolled beside the Seine River; fat burghers and their plump wives waddled comfortably down Berlin's Unter den Linden. Royal guardsmen in bearskin hats and scarlet tunics stood watch outside Buckingham Palace.

That June, American tourists crossed the Atlantic in record numbers. Europe's hotel keepers never before had enjoyed better business. There was dancing, laughter and gaiety. Champagne corks popped even as the cadenced beat of marching men grew louder on the cobblestones of old cities.

Leaving Berlin for London, Colonel House told newsmen, "I believe Europe is a tinder box. It needs only a spark to set the whole thing off."

3

BLACK AUGUST

AMERICANS, SAVE THOSE OF EUROPEAN EXTRACTION, PAID
little attention to the affair in Sarajevo. "It's too bad about
that Austrian duke and his wife," a well-known newspaper
columnist wrote. "But, really, we don't give a good hoot for
royalty or Europe's troubles. We're more interested in the
National League pennant race. . . ."

Actually, the event was too remote, the dangers too obscure,
for Americans to become alarmed. "The whole business will
be forgotten in six weeks," a mid-western congressman predicted. "The thing for us to do is tend our own shop and
keep out of European business."

That summer, Americans by the thousands were saving
money to buy an automobile—most probably a Model T
Ford, the fabulous "Tin Lizzie" or "flivver." Henry Ford's
rattletrap cars were fast becoming familiar sights on the
bumpy, dusty 1914 United States roads. Let them rave about
war over there in Europe. Americans raved about sensible
things such as flivvers.

Mr. Ford, who manufactured the cars in his Detroit plant,
had recently "set the country on its ear" by introducing a
revolutionary wage scale for his employees—five dollars per
day. This was an incredible salary at a time when factory
workers were receiving only ten dollars or less for a week's
work.

"I believe in a fair day's pay for a fair day's work," Ford
had stated.

However, Ford's fellow capitalists did not take to his economic theories. Instead, they continued paying out low wages and, when workers struck in protest, spent fortunes to hire scabs, guards and "goons" to break the walkouts.

Coinciding with the European war scare were great labor struggles in the United States. Headlines on domestic industrial turmoil overshadowed the news from Europe. One strike, by coal miners in Ludlow, Colorado, resulted in such violence that President Wilson sent Regular Army troops to quell the disorder. Wilson, a Democrat, had been elected with labor support and was now bitterly criticized by his former backers.

A man who espoused peace, Wilson risked war with Mexico in 1914 by rushing Marines and warships to Vera Cruz after United States sailors had been beaten there by a mob of anti-American demonstrators.

Wilson demanded that Mexico pay indemnities and also honor the American flag with a twenty-one gun salute. When this was rejected by the Mexican government, Marines stormed ashore and seized Vera Cruz. Many Mexicans and nineteen Americans were slain in the brief fighting.

Soon after, a revolution flared in Mexico against the dictatorial regime of President Victoriano Huerta. The United States backed insurgent General Venustiano Carranza, who finally became President. No sooner had he been installed than a fresh anti-American threat arose. General Francisco (Pancho) Villa rebelled against Carranza, whom he labeled a tool of the "Gringos." ("Gringo" was a contemptuous term used to describe people from the United States.) Villa rallied a large following sworn to wipe out Gringo influence in Mexico. He was a reckless desperado and frequently launched raids across the Rio Grande onto American soil, especially in New Mexico.

Thus, many matters besides the European crisis occupied

Americans. Included was public indignation over paying an income tax to the federal government in compliance with the recently adopted Sixteenth Amendment to the Constitution. It was easier to start a heated argument about the income tax than the European troubles.

But New World aloofness did not lessen Old World tension. Angry exchanges passed between Vienna and Belgrade, the Serbian capital. For a week after Franz Ferdinand's death, the Austrian press thundered against the Serbs. However, Count Leopold von Berchtold, the Austrian Foreign Minister, carefully avoided committing his country to any irrevocable action. Although the newspapers beat the war drums, the Chief of Staff, General Conrad von Hotzendorff, did not order even a limited mobilization.

Emperor Franz Josef remained in seclusion, apparently mourning his nephew. Actually, the aged monarch was awaiting word from Germany before issuing any statement on Austrian action. The Emperor was not concerned about making war on Serbia; Franz Josef was satisfied that his armies could quickly smash that country. But he knew Russia would become involved and did not care to tackle the Tsar's forces unless assured of German help.

The question of war or peace in Europe hinged upon Germany. On July 5, von Berchtold sent an emissary to Berlin at the request of the Kaiser, who wanted to make his stand clear.

Wilhelm advised the Austrian delegate that Germany would back her ally to the limit no matter what course Franz Josef decided to follow. "Take any path you please. War or peace. It matters not to us. We shall support you either way to the last full measure," the Kaiser declared.

Having handed the Austrians "a blank check, valid against the whole resources of the German Empire, to fill out at pleasure," a contemporary historian wrote, the Kaiser left aboard the royal yacht for a three-week cruise among the Norwegian fjords, while Austria toyed with the world's fate.

In mid-July, von Berchtold and his cabinet met with Franz Josef. The old Emperor decided the course of history. Von Berchtold asked, "Now that Germany has pledged to help us, do you agree to war against Serbia, sire?" The Emperor faltered only a moment. "I do," he said, thus dooming millions of innocent people.

The road to war was open, but Austria still had to play out the ritual of diplomacy. On July 23, von Berchtold dispatched a harsh note to Serbia listing a number of outrageous demands, including an admission by Serbia that her officials were participating in anti-Austrian conspiracies.

The Austrians also wanted their police to have free rein on Serbian soil to put down subversion against the Austro-Hungarian Empire. In addition, the investigation of the Sarajevo murders was to be carried out by Austrian agents inside Serbia; if the culprits were apprehended, they must be tried before judges appointed by Emperor Franz Josef's Minister of Justice.

The note contained other humiliating features. It had purposely been so worded that its acceptance was most unlikely. In a reply that reached Vienna on July 25, the Serbs accepted almost every demand. The only exceptions taken were to the clauses about Austrian police and judges.

"No nation could maintain its sovereignty under such conditions," King Peter of Serbia protested. He suggested that these questions be submitted for arbitration to the International Tribunal at The Hague or to an impartial commission.

The Serbs, obviously wanting to placate Austria, were willing to make almost every concession. Von Berchtold was both surprised and disappointed. He had not anticipated an answer of this sort. When Kaiser Wilhelm of Germany heard the news, he said to the Austrian ambassador in Berlin, "You have won a great moral victory—but I suggest you act at once; ignore the Serbian note and make war."

The Serbs probably had anticipated this Austrian reaction, for Marshal Radomir Putnik ordered full mobilization at 3:00 P.M., July 25, even as the conciliatory note was being delivered to Vienna.

Serbian military preparations gave von Berchtold the excuse for action. He ordered the Austro-Hungarian ambassador to leave Belgrade and at 9:23 P.M., July 25, persuaded Emperor Franz Josef to alert the single army corps that General von Hotzendorff thought was needed to crush the Serbs.

The war tides were sweeping across Europe. However, Sir Edward Grey, the British Foreign Secretary, still sought to have the quarrel mediated, and Count Theobald von Bethmann-Hollweg, the German Chancellor, hypocritically talked of "localizing" hostilities.

Matters had gone beyond mediation, and the situation was too explosive for a "local" war. The Doomsday Hour had struck.

Austria declared war on Serbia on Tuesday, July 28, 1914. Her troops jauntily marched across the border and by the twenty-ninth, shells were falling in Belgrade from Austrian gunboats in the Danube River. As Austrian and Serbian guns fired the opening shots of World War I, the spotlight shifted from Vienna and Belgrade to St. Petersburg where, on July 30, the Russian Tsar signed an order for general mobilization. Hordes of Russian troops began gathering at the Russo-Austrian frontiers.

The wheel spun faster. As Russia mobilized, Germany made her move. On Friday, July 31, the Kaiser gave the Tsar twelve hours in which to demobilize. At the same time, he issued an ultimatum demanding to know whether France would stay neutral in a Russo-German conflict.

The German ambassador to France was instructed that should he receive a favorable reply, the French must hand over to Germany as a pledge the fortresses of Toul and Verdun. This was an impossible stipulation and the Germans knew it. The Kaiser was determined to have his war.

Meanwhile, the British Royal Navy's Home Fleet, which had been on maneuvers, concentrated along the Kentish coast. All leaves were canceled in the British Army, and England was placed on a war alert basis.

The Kaiser had sound reasons to press for war at that particular time. The Triple Entente was plagued with serious domestic troubles. Crippling strikes, fomented by revolutionaries, were spreading throughout Russia. England faced an insurrection in southern Ireland, where the people were demanding freedom, and France was torn by riots over a sensational murder trial involving the wife of a cabinet minister.

The Continent sweltered in a heat wave that sent the thermometer over 100 degrees, but the August weather did not match the raging international fever. Saturday, August 1, Germany declared war on Russia, which had not demobilized in accordance with the Kaiser's warning. The same day, France rejected the German demands and ordered general mobilization, a step followed immediately by the Germans.

After debating all week end, the Kaiser's government formally declared war upon France on Tuesday, August 3. Prior to this, and in violation of international guarantees, German forces had entered Luxembourg at 9:00 P.M., Saturday, August 1, to seize the railroad lines they needed for shipping troops and supplies to the West.

The Kaiser also sent a note to Belgium demanding of King Albert I the free passage of German troops to attack France. The only excuse the Germans made was the flimsy one that the French were planning to violate Belgian neutrality and the Kaiser wanted to "save" that little nation from such "excesses."

Albert, King of the Belgians, was a brave and resolute monarch. Instead of backing down before the Germans, he warned them that he would fight to preserve his nation's integrity and a long-standing neutrality guaranteed jointly in a treaty signed by Germany, Austria, Hungary, France, Russia and Great Britain.

When twelve regiments of Uhlans crossed the Belgian border near Liege on August 4, King Albert appealed to France and Great Britain for help. The French responded at once, and the British government decided to stick by its commitments to Belgium.

During the afternoon of Tuesday, August 4, Sir Edward Goschen, Britain's minister to Berlin, warned that unless German troops were withdrawn from Belgian soil by midnight his country would declare war.

Von Bethmann-Hollweg had already admitted Germany's guilt in the invasion of Belgium by saying, ". . . it is a wrong we will try to make good as soon as our military ends have been reached." Yet when Goschen presented the British ultimatum, the German Chancellor angrily cried, "Would you go to war over a scrap of paper?"

The treaty was more than a "scrap of paper" to England. German troops continued to press forward in Belgium. At midnight, August 4, the British Prime Minister, Herbert Henry Asquith, solemnly announced that a state of war existed between his country and Germany.

4

"ATTACK! ATTACK! ALWAYS THE ATTACK!"

IN VIENNA AND BERLIN THE OUTBREAK OF WAR WAS GREETED with jubilation. German reservists marched along streets lined by singing, cheering spectators. The troops in *feld-grau* (field gray) uniforms and spiked helmets were pelted with flowers thrown from rooftops and balconies. *"Deutschland, Deutschland über Alles!"* the marchers sang.

"Nach Paris!" roared the crowds. "On to Paris!"

The German soldiers tramped to the railroad depots with flowers in their rifle muzzles. The goose-stepping soldiers strode on with arrogant precision. The mighty German Army was a relentless machine, rank after rank of human robots in drab *feld-grau*.

To an onlooker "the outpouring of military might passing through Berlin was awesome . . . ." And that was only one city. All over Germany the clatter of cavalry, the rattling of artillery caissons, the thundering cadence of marching men, drowned out all other sounds.

Now the war was reality. Everywhere it touched off mass hysteria. Mobs poured down the boulevards of Paris to gather in teeming thousands at the Arc de Triomphe in a spontaneous patriotic outburst. The strains of "La Marseillaise" rose skyward like a fervent hymn.

The French, clad in their traditional blue jackets and red

trousers of the 1870's, *képis* jauntily cocked on their heads, went out to meet the enemy.

"À Berlin!" cried the people. "On to Berlin!" The time had come to get even with *les salles boches* and win back Alsace and Lorraine. This was a holy war for the French. A war fed by forty years of smoldering hatreds.

Even the usually phlegmatic English entered the conflict with a spasm of emotion. The "Old Contemptibles" of the Regular Army marched off with professional zeal. Tommy Atkins was earning his soldier's pay again. Down London's Regent Street he went, rifle at the slope, eyes front, arms swinging. The Scottish regiments wearing traditional kilts tramped to the piers and docks with bagpipes skirling and colors snapping under cloudy English skies.

So the people of Europe went to war, with cheering and singing, with prayers and tears. In St. Petersburg (soon to be renamed Petrograd) huge masses of people gathered outside the palace to greet the Tsar, and when he appeared on the balcony in view of his subjects, a shout went up "like the roar of a mighty ocean," a newspaperman wrote. In Moscow and Kiev, in the towns and the villages of Tsarist Russia, the churches were crowded and the bearded priests intoned blessings on kneeling men in uniform.

The armies of Russia plodded to the borders and the soldiers swore allegiance to the "Little Father"—the Tsar. Who was to know in the August days of 1914 that Tsar Nicholas would be the last of the Romanoffs to rule Russia?

Who then guessed the despotism of Tsarism was fated to be replaced by the despotism of Lenin, Trotsky, Stalin and Khrushchev?

The Russian Revolution was still more than three years off, and the soldiers trodding across the sun-baked Russian and Polish land did not yet waver in their loyalty to the Tsar.

They had to be sacrificed by the thousands in futile battles before the whispers of revolt rose to thunder in their ears.

The war, which seemed so distant and unreal back in the United States, assumed nightmarish vividness for nearly 20,000 American tourists caught up in the conflict on the Continent.

Since many ship sailings were suddenly canceled, thousands were left stranded. The safest place, it seemed to everyone, was England, separated from the warring nations by the width of the Channel.

Some cross-Channel shuttle boats remained in operation, but it was difficult to reach the ports from cities like Berlin, Vienna, Budapest or Moscow. Railroads were taken over by the military authorities of the various countries, and travelers were hard put to find transportation to Calais, Ostend, Dunkirk or The Hook of Holland, which were the main Channel ports.

Many Americans, unable to get out, were left penniless as the price of food in restaurants and the cost of hotel rooms soared. The United States embassies in all the capitals were besieged by anxious tourists pleading for help.

President Wilson acted at once. On August 6, he announced United States neutrality in the conflict and then moved to help the war-stranded Americans. The cruiser *Tennessee,* carrying $7,500,000, was rushed to Le Havre, France, where American agents distributed the sum to United States embassies, which received orders to "deny no American citizen financial and material aid." Loans up to $1,000 were authorized.

The U. S. Navy arranged a fleet of transports to carry Americans home from designated ports—Le Havre and Cherbourg in France, Plymouth and Southampton in England. Most Americans took advantage of this chance to leave Europe, but some remained, especially those who had been living in Paris, where a large American colony flourished. Scores of expatriates enlisted in the French Army and fought as individuals. Two years later American fliers formed the famous Lafayette Escadrille.

As tourists fled the Continent for England or the United States, the war started in earnest. The German invasion of Belgium was no impromptu maneuver, but part of a well-conceived plan originated in 1907 by General Graf Alfred von Schlieffen, formerly chief of the German General Staff.

Von Schlieffen had died in 1912 at the age of eighty, but his scheme for conquest, with some modifications, was used by the Germans in 1914. The "von Schlieffen Plan" was based on the premise that Germany would have to fight on two fronts, against Russia in the East and France and Great Britain in the West.

Von Schlieffen coined the term *blitzkrieg* (lightning war) to describe his technique for defeating Germany's western enemies. An attack from Germany against France's strongly fortified border would be disastrous, he stated. The French forts from Belfort to Verdun were "impregnable." The thing to do was to go around them in a sweeping end run through Belgium and southern Holland, thus outflanking the French defensive system.

According to von Schlieffen, the "strong right wing" of the German armies would "pursue the enemy relentlessly" and then "cut like a scythe," to entrap the enemy between the Swiss border and their own forts.

One of the basic factors in von Schlieffen's master plan was his understanding of the French doctrine of war. He knew the enemy was committed to a philosophy of attack and anticipated an offensive into Alsace-Lorraine should hostilities occur.

Such action by the French would facilitate the German sweep through Belgium and into France, for it would weaken the French resistance on the right and waste men and matériel in a futile assault.

The credo of the French Army was *"Attaque! Attaque! Toujours l'attaque!"* (Attack! Attack! Always the attack!)

It was preached at the St. Cyr Military Academy by fanatical, fiery-eyed Colonel de Grandmaison, who cried out to the young officer cadets: "For the attack only two things are necessary: to know where the enemy is and to decide what to do. What the enemy intends to do is of no consequence."

Incredibly, Grandmaison's superiors let him teach this military madness. The French Army, trained in bayonet fighting, had spirit and courage, but the bayonet was useless against machine guns, quick-firing rifles and modern artillery. The machine gun, which had never before been widely used in warfare, was now the ruler of the battlefield. The Germans recognized its value, and their gunners were the world's best trained.

Somehow, the French General Staff did not understand that the day was gone when armies needed nothing more than brave officers and men. The French soldiers in their horizon blue uniforms and red pants were ready for war as it had been fought in 1870, not 1914.

France would have to sacrifice thousands of her sons before her generals could be made to understand that the machine gun was superior to the bayonet. This was true of the British generals as well, and only when they learned that lesson were the Germans made to pay for the arrogant ambitions that had loosed the dogs of war.

5

THE DAYS OF BLOOD AND SORROW

GENERAL VON SCHLIEFFEN'S BLUEPRINT WAS CHANGED BY HIS successor, General Helmuth von Moltke, nephew of the man who had crushed France in 1870. Because von Moltke feared that the Dutch might flood the lowlands and impede his advance, he eliminated the invasion of Holland. Fretful that the expected French invasion of Germany might push too far, he cut down the size of his right wing to bolster the German border defense. He felt that not enough troops faced the Russians in the East and sent more than four corps there from the western front.

These alterations of the von Schlieffen Plan still left two tremendous forces totaling some fifty-five divisions to carry out the wheeling movement through Belgium. The First Army under General Alexander von Kluck and the Second Army (General Karl von Bülow) had to break through the ring of Belgian forts around Liege and establish bridgeheads across the Meuse River with a minimum of delay.

Liege was defended by a ring of twelve forts which had been built in the 1890's. They were manned by some 40,000 men whose commanding officer, General Gerard Leman, was a brilliant and devoted soldier.

King Albert, in a handwritten note to Leman, exhorted the general: "I charge you to hold to the end . . . the position which you have been entrusted to defend."

General Leman and his men tried their best. On the night of August 5–6, the Germans attacked. They were beaten back with heavy losses, although the city of Liege fell when the fleeing Germans were rallied by General Erich Ludendorff, a Second Army staff officer destined for future fame.

The capture of Liege was only a steppingstone for the Germans. They had to take the Belgian forts before the *blitzkrieg* could be carried out. The Liege forts were obsolescent. Their armored turrets could withstand only an eight-inch shell. The bastions had heavy guns mounted in steel cupolas which rose to fire and sank down to reload. Although this procedure was slow and clumsy, the guns of the fortresses blocked the advance.

The Germans sent out a call for heavy siege howitzers, and mammoth seventeen-inch cannon made at the Krupp works were dragged to the battle zone. The monsters hurled shells which demolished the fortified positions and cracked the steel turrets like walnuts. Even so, the Belgians fought on at Liege until August 16 and held out two days longer at Namur; but nothing could withstand the great siege guns, and the Germans moved forward.

The Belgian government fled from Brussels to Antwerp, and the Germans entered the capital on August 20. An American observer watched them enter.

> They came like machines rather than men. The grayness of their uniforms matched the gray stones of the buildings and all merged together into a great mass. There was no sound but the *clomp, clomp, clomp* of German jackboots on the cobblestones; the clatter of artillery wheels and the horses' hooves. The people of Brussels lined the curbs and stared in silence; no one moved, not even a baby whimpered . . . and from the watching throngs rose a mute hatred, unspoken, unseen and yet real.

All that day the Germans marched through Brussels, and all through the night. Regiment after regiment, always in cadenced step, always in alignment. The Germans showed neither joy nor elation in the Belgian capital; they marched on, eyes to the fore, heading toward the French border.

A newspaperman wrote:

> . . . the weather was hot, and when the last Germans had passed, the smell of sweat from thousands of men lingered behind them. I saw a Belgian housewife carry a pail of soapy water into the street, get down on her hands and knees and scrub the stones as if to cleanse them of the invaders.

The main Belgian army retreated to the forts at Antwerp and the way into France was open to the Germans. But as the Kaiser's forces won military victories in Belgium, anti-German feeling began rising in the world because of German tactics in the drive through Belgium.

Belgian civilians were treated with brutality. The roads soon became clogged as refugees fled the invaders. The German advance was marked by vandalism. Protests showered into Berlin when von Kluck's troops destroyed Europe's finest rare book collections by burning the internationally famous Louvain Library.

"The German conquerors are behaving like uncivilized Huns!" An American war correspondent wrote from Louvain.

As the enemy drove onward, the French behaved as far-seeing von Schlieffen had predicted. Instead of rushing troops northward to check the Germans, they hurled a headlong assault into Alsace-Lorraine.

Massed horizon-blue-clad infantry regiments charged at the Germans, flags to the fore, sunlight glinting off their long bayonets. They were cut down like ripened wheat by enemy machine guns.

After ghastly losses the French briefly gained a foothold in Alsace-Lorraine. They entered the border towns amid emotional scenes as weeping civilians embraced the soldiers of France and cheered the red-white-and-blue tricolor which fluttered over Alsace-Lorraine soil for the first time since 1871. It did not remain long. Within a week, a German counterthrust expelled the French army from Alsace and Lorraine.

For eleven days (August 14–25) fighting raged without a halt from Belgium to the Swiss border. More than 3,500,000 troops were involved in a series of engagements known as the Battles of the Frontiers.

The Germans inflicted over 300,000 casualties on the French, but the invaders also suffered, particularly when they came against elements of the 150,000-man British Expeditionary Force which had landed at Le Havre, Ostend and Dunkirk on August 7.

The "Old Contemptibles," led by Field Marshal Sir John French, an irascible sixty-one-year-old soldier, went into action near Mons, Belgium, where von Kluck's fast-moving First Army attacked a British corps of 30,000 which was holding defensive positions.

The Battle of Mons, which began on Sunday, August 23, ended in a British defeat, but that day, the Germans learned to respect Tommy Atkins. Field Marshal French's riflemen were so effective that a German regimental commander, whose unit was almost wiped out as it led the attack, reported to First Army headquarters: ". . . I am convinced the English have 20 machine guns per battalion. . . . Never have I seen such firepower. . . . My shock troops were killed by scores."

The German colonel was wrong. There were only two

machine guns in a British battalion. The torrent of lead had poured from Enfield rifles handled by Tommy Atkins. No conscript army could ever attain the skill and proficiency of the "Old Contemptibles." They would have prevailed at Mons, but lacked sufficient numbers, and von Kluck pushed them back only by sheer weight.

The Battles of the Frontiers ended during the last week of August, and the German armies poured into France at Lille.

In less than a month's fighting, the Germans had hammered out victory enough to win most past wars. By all standards the French Army should have been ready to quit. The retreating troops fell back in the dust and heat with the relentless Germans at their heels.

However, neither the French, the British nor the Belgians (who still fought from the fortress city of Antwerp) cracked. Defeat steeled national resolve to resist the German war machine. The troops who had blunted the Prussian onslaught marched day and night in a blur of fatigue. Mounted men dozed in the saddle and often toppled to the ground. But discipline was maintained; squads, companies, battalions, regiments and divisions remained intact despite calamitous losses.

Any prisoners the Germans captured had to be taken in combat. No large numbers of discouraged and demoralized men gave up voluntarily. The British and French did not abandon their guns or equipment along the line of retreat. These were the signs of broken armies. Troops that stayed together and kept their weapons could still fight.

"What must we do to make the French see they are defeated?" von Moltke complained to a subordinate. He was a man with limited understanding who could not quite grasp anything unusual. According to military doctrine, armies that were consistently beaten in battle lost morale. When this happened they surrendered *en masse.* But this did not take place on the western front.

The German commander-in-chief was upset by the unorthodox behavior of the British and French. But his confusion changed to near panic when he heard that the Russians had won a big victory and entered East Prussia. Instead of waiting to learn how seriously the Russians threatened his homeland, von Moltke disregarded von Schlieffin's advice to "keep the right wing strong" and detached two corps each from both the First and Second Armies.

These troops he rushed to the eastern front. Military historians consider von Moltke's move as a "fatal blunder." Every German soldier was needed in the West if the *blitzkrieg* was to succeed. By depriving them of four corps, von Moltke had weakened his right wing enough to end all hope of swift triumph over France and Britain.

But this was not yet evident to the German people. Back in the Fatherland, optimism and enthusiasm blotted out the casualty lists. Too bad that so many fine young men had to fall in battle, the Germans reasoned. However, their sacrifice was not in vain.

Soon, the enemy must surrender. What a glorious day that would be for Germany! While the grief of a nation could never restore to life those who had bought the victory with their blood, it was every German's duty to die for the Fatherland if necessary.

The Kaiser had told them theirs was a holy cause. "God is with us!" he had declared. "The spirit of God has descended upon me, the German Emperor. . . . I am His Sword, His weapon!"

A quasi-religious fervor swept Germany. The people looked upon the Kaiser as a divine figure. God was with the Germans and nothing could harm them. However, some were not so reverent. A cynical joke made the rounds in Berlin: "Of course God is with us. He's always on the side that has the heaviest artillery!"

The smugly confident Germans daily awaited word of total victory. But as that bloody August dragged along and Europe sweated under the worst heat in a century, the Germans grew more annoyed than concerned when the fighting continued to rage furiously in the West.

Sudden anxiety gripped them when the Russians shattered an Austrian army and smashed through the German troops to invade both Austrian-held Galicia and East Prussia. It was incredible that Russian peasants could defeat Germans. The huge Russian armies lurched forward in East Prussia. Königsberg fell and other centers were threatened. Then, the Germans struck back. Led by General Paul von Hindenburg, whose chief of staff was General Erich Ludendorff, the *Reichswehr* (German Army), entrapped the Russians at Tannenberg in East Prussia. The battle lasted three days (August 27–30) to end in a massive victory for von Hindenburg. Great numbers of Russians were killed, wounded or missing; 125,000 were captured and an entire Tsarist army demolished.

General Alexander Samsonov, the Russian commander, committed suicide. His last words were: "The Tsar trusted me and I failed him."

Tannenberg eased the Russian threat in the East, although the Tsar's armies still presented a formidable threat, particularly in Galicia, where the Austrians were fighting for their lives.

So far the Austro-Hungarian effort had been a great disappointment. The commander, General Conrad von Hotzendorff, was a brilliant soldier, but his armies did not match their leader. The Austro-Hungarian forces were made up of ten different nationalities. Many soldiers understood no German except for eighty words of command. The defects in the Austro-Hungarian armies were soon exposed.

Instead of gaining swift victory against the Serbs, they were hurled back by General Radomir Putnik and his hardy soldiers at the Drina River, where thousands of Austrians were killed, wounded or captured.

General von Hotzendorff fared no better against Russia. He lost so many men in the opening weeks of the war that a German staff officer bitterly remarked, "We have no allies. We are shackled to a corpse."

The Germans regarded themselves as a superior race with all the virtues and no faults. They could not or would not admit that Germany's enemies were equally brave and patriotic.

The setbacks suffered in France by the British Expeditionary Forces seemed to stiffen the people at home. Young men swamped recruiting offices in the rush to join the colors. Factory workers put in long hours grinding out the tools of war. "Stop the Hun!" became the national slogan.

In France, the masses echoed a stirring cry: *"Ils ne passerent pass!"* (They shall not pass!) Frenchmen and women pressed the fight against *les salles boches* in every city, town and village. The tricolor flew from housetops and windows. "Never has there been such an outburst of patriotism. Now, as the *boches* descend upon us, we shall prove ourselves worthy of being Frenchmen," a Paris journalist wrote.

Humble village churches and magnificent cathedrals all over the land were crowded daily with worshippers praying for a miracle. August waned and the guns rumbled ever nearer Paris. Von Moltke's armies trampled over the blooming fields of northern France and crossed rivers into ancient cities where age-old buildings were pounded to rubble as the Germans cut a swath of devastation in their relentless march. *"Nach Paris!"* von Kluck and von Bülow ordered their men. French prayers had apparently fallen on deaf ears. No one knew it, but a miracle was in the offing. It would be performed at the Marne River only twenty miles from Paris, in the September sunshine amid wild flowers growing along the banks of the lovely river.

6

THE MIRACLE AT THE MARNE

As THE INEXORABLE GERMAN TIDE ROLLED ACROSS FRANCE, THE war's backwash reached to every corner of the world. At sea, the Royal Navy fought an inconclusive engagement off Helgoland Bight with the Germans.

Several German raiders slipped through the British blockade to ravage Allied shipping. The most notorious of these ships was the *Emden*, which ranged into the Indian Ocean where she preyed on British and French merchantmen.

The shock waves of the war were felt in Africa. There the British quickly conquered German Togoland and invaded the Cameroons. In Asia, Japan entered the war against Germany (August 22) and immediately seized the German-held Caroline and Marshall Islands in the Pacific. On the Asian mainland, the Japanese laid siege to Tsingtao, a German colony of China. The Mikado's Navy scoured the Pacific for German submarines and surface raiders.

At first the war brought a reaction in the United States best summarized by an editorial on the front page of a midwestern newspaper: "We never appreciated so keenly as now the foresight exercised by our forefathers in migrating from Europe." However, the callous invasion of Belgium soon aroused heated anti-German sentiments all over the nation. Since Americans traditionally took the side of the underdog, their sympathies were with Belgium. Officially, the United States adopted a policy of neutrality. President Wilson had announced this position on August 6, at the same time offering to act as arbitrator in the conflict.

Protected by a 3,000-mile span of ocean, America could stand apart from the ghastly slaughter raging on the battlefields of Europe where the fighting reached a climax in the West by September 2. It was clear that only a military miracle could save France. The French government left Paris for Bordeaux as the Germans pressed unchecked to the Marne River.

To General Joseph Gallieni, a tough old soldier with a combat record earned in North Africa, went the responsibility of defending Paris. Gallieni was the man for the job. He issued a stirring proclamation to the troops under his command: "Stand fast, comrades! Make Paris a German tomb!"

Gallieni did more than deliver speeches. He set everyone to work digging trenches and erecting roadblocks outside Paris. He forced civilians to do this work with pick and shovel.

Weapons were handed out to all who could carry them, and Paris was turned into an armed camp. Cafés were boarded up and deserted. Grim-faced soldiers and civil militia guarded street barricades. Gallieni declared: "If *les boches* take our beloved city, let them find only corpses among its ashes! We shall fight to the last man and the last cartridge! *Vive la patrie!*"

The last-ditch defense of Paris had been decided on by the commander-in-chief of the French Army, General Joseph Jacques Joffre, who was called "Papa" Joffre because he always referred to his soldiers as *"mes enfants"* (my children).

With his scraggly white mustache and heavy paunch, Joffre looked more like a genial innkeeper than a soldier. Although no brilliant general, he was capable. Papa Joffre let nothing disturb him. Brave and determined, he was slow to act, but

once he decided on a course, nothing could deter him from
it.

"We will stop the Germans" he reassured his staff on
September 2 as President Raymond Poincaré and other government leaders were entraining for Bordeaux. At that
moment, no gambler would have backed Joffre. Von Kluck's
First Army had reached the Marne River and at one point
stood only twenty miles from Paris. The situation was grim
for France. Gallieni rushed every man to meet the Germans.

Von Kluck's patrols ran into resistance at the Marne. On
September 5 the great battle began in a flurry of rifle shots.
Joffre rushed more units into the fighting, and German rein-
forcements hurried to the front.

The fighting raged for five days along a 100-mile front. It
was a seesaw struggle. Neither army had ever fought harder.
During one phase of the engagement, General Ferdinand
Foch, commanding the French Ninth Army, sent a dispatch
to Joffre: "Hard pressed on my right. My center is yielding.
Impossible to maneuver. Situation excellent. I attack." This
message symbolized the French spirit at the Marne.

For a time on September 7–8, German advance units came
so close to Paris that they could see the Eiffel Tower and the
spires of the city. General Gallieni gathered all taxicabs in
the city and loaded them with soldiers. With horns beeping,
the taxis rattled to the front. The taxicabs of Paris saved the
day in this first automobile movement ever of troops to a
battlefield.

After nearly a week, the miracle for which the French had
entreated took place. On September 9, von Moltke ordered a
retreat to the Aisne River. Now the Germans tasted defeat;
it affected them strangely. Inside Germany, the civilians flew
into a mass fury at the news. Newspaper offices were stoned by
irate mobs for carrying stories of the setback at the Marne.

The Marne and Aisne Area

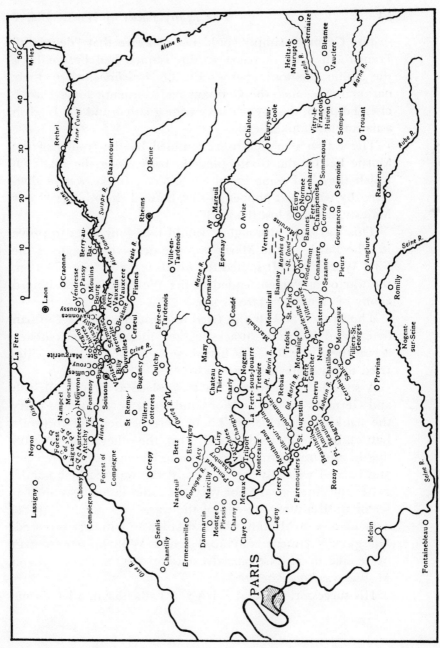

The Germans simply could not conceive that "decadent" Frenchmen and "mercenary" Englishmen had beaten back the noble Teutonic heroes of the *Reichswehr*. In their national arrogance the Germans had contempt for everyone else. To them, the French were wine guzzlers and the English a nation of shopkeepers.

The Kaiser's soldiers were stunned by the results of the Marne battle; the troops plodded back along the roads on which they had come in triumph. Von Moltke was so shattered by what had happened that he told the Kaiser: "Your Majesty, we have lost the war!"

This was true, although it would take four years to prove it. The Battle of the Marne was the decisive struggle of the First World War. It stalled the *blitzkrieg,* and from then on, the war of movement ended in the West and the prolonged agony of trench warfare began.

The French and British tried to capitalize on the German defeat and launched attacks against the enemy entrenched across the Aisne River. When these were repulsed, the Allies tried to outflank the foe.

A so-called race to the sea took place as French, British and Germans moved divisions and corps northward to parry the flanking movements. There were clashes and full-scale battles, but neither side could break the other. The infantry dug in and northern France soon became a maze of trenches and barbed wire. By September 18 the war reached a stalemate; the lines would not vary ten miles either way in that sector until almost the end of the war.

General von Moltke, who had failed to win, was replaced. His gloomy lament convinced Kaiser Wilhelm a new man must take over. The official excuse given for relieving von Moltke was "poor health."

His successor, General Erich von Falkenhayn, a handsome

fifty-three-year-old infantry officer, had been serving as the Prussian Minister of War when the call came. He took over in the West with a sure hand and proved to be a first-class leader.

The French also made top-level shifts. General Ferdinand Foch became Papa Joffre's chief aide. Virtually placed in charge of the "race to the sea," Foch showed himself to be a brilliant tactician. Although his sharp tongue and quick temper sparked dissension with British and Belgian generals, Foch was essentially honest and loyal.

Only two more major developments took place on the western front during 1914. At the end of September, the Germans brought heavy siege guns to bear against Antwerp. The nineteenth-century fortresses surrounding the city were pulverized until October 6, when King Albert could no longer hold out because Antwerp's civilian population panicked.

The valiant King saved his army in a four-day withdrawal. The Germans entered battered Antwerp on October 10, but the Belgians had won a moral victory by keeping thousands of enemy troops busy for weeks.

Eager to resume the offensive, General von Falkenhayn thought he could force a breakthrough at Ypres in Flanders, which was held by a thin line of British and Belgian troops. Young German volunteer shock regiments charged the foe with senseless fury.

"They advanced, singing, to their deaths," an incredulous correspondent noted. These assault units were annihilated. The British, aided by French and Belgians, then loosed a counteroffensive. The month-long attack at Ypres (which Tommy Atkins pronounced "Wipers") ground to a standstill in the Flanders mud on November 12.

Men died by the thousands in the slime and filth. The

trenches were dug more deeply. The barbed wire was strung like intricately woven spider webs. In the West, 1914 ended without any final decision, although the Germans held much of industrial France. More than 500,000 Frenchmen had become casualties. The British Regular Army was practically wiped out. The Belgians clung to only a corner of their country. But the Germans had lost their chance for a quick victory. They, too, suffered enormous numbers of dead and wounded. The combatants were like heavyweight fighters who had punched themselves into mutual exhaustion and now clinched for breath.

In the East, the Tsarist armies had been merely staggered, not crushed, at Tannenberg and proved it by practically annihilating an Austrian army in Galicia and Poland, although German counteroffensives finally halted the Russian thrusts. The hapless Austrians were also beaten in Serbia during December, when the "snow was red with Austrian blood."

Turkey entered the war on the side of Germany in October, opening other fronts—the Middle East and Caucasia. The Turks provided little help. The British fought them in Mesopotamia and won, while the Russians scored a great success in the Caucasian Mountains, where an entire Turkish corps was eliminated.

The navies grappled and clashed in the Atlantic. A German victory over the British off the coast of Chile was avenged on December 8, near the Falkland Islands, when the Royal Navy wiped out the triumphant enemy cruiser squadron.

German surface raiders swooped on Allied shipping, but their best ships, the *Karlsruhe* and the *Emden,* were sunk. The former blew up off Barbados when an ammunition magazine caught fire, and the *Emden* was pounded to pieces by the Australian cruiser *Sydney,* near the Cocos Islands.

As 1914 faded into history, the skies over much of the world flamed red with the fires of war. The voices that greeted the New Year in Europe were not raised in celebration. They were the shrieks of the wounded and the dying. The world writhed in torment, and a wail of grief arose from widows, orphans, mothers and fathers in the war-torn lands.

PART TWO

« 1915–1916 »
THE BATTERING RAM

Take up our quarrel with the foe:
To you from falling hands we throw
The torch; be yours to hold it high.
If ye break faith with us who die
We shall not sleep, though poppies grow
In Flanders fields.
JOHN McRAE, *In Flanders Fields,* 1915

1

THE PLAN THAT FAILED

To the world, Russia was known as "The Bear That Walks Like A Man." This phrase aptly described the lumbering Russian armies which tackled the Germans and Austrians with ursine courage. Somehow, after five months of unrelenting warfare, the badly led, poorly equipped Tsarist troops still faced the enemy, despite the terrible slaughter of Tannenberg and other battles.

Theoretically, the Allies had not fared too badly on the eastern front. Only the Germans managed to win victories against Russia. Austria's armies had suffered gravely in both Russia and Serbia. At the start of 1915, the Tsar's forces occupied more Austrian territory than the Germans held of Russian soil.

Nevertheless, Russia was in serious trouble. She was drained by the 1914 fighting that had cost many thousands of casualties. Russian losses were astronomical; the Germans took more than 750,000 prisoners alone. But the Tsar still had a tremendous human reservoir from which to refill his armies. Russia's problem was equipment, not manpower.

Since the outbreak of war, Russian artillery had fired thirty times as many shells as the nation's arsenals could produce. Her stockpile of ammunition was nearly gone.

More than a million rifles had been lost in combat, and in some regiments only one man in three was armed. Shortages of such basic weapons as machine guns, hand grenades and sidearms plagued Russia. She lacked everything from shoes to bayonets and fieldpieces.

A Russian collapse loomed in 1915 when it became obvious that the Germans could detach whole divisions from the stalemated trench warfare in the West. The Kaiser's generals had learned that a comparatively few men, well supplied with automatic weapons, could hold a line of trenches against even the heaviest attacks.

If England and France expected the Tsar to stay in the war, they had to provide immediate substantial aid. But with Turkey on the German side, British and French ships were barred from the most direct route to Russia, which was through the Dardanelles to the Sea of Marmara and the Black Sea port of Odessa.

The German high command, aware that Russia was weakening, planned to knock her out of the war by a massive attack to be launched in the spring of 1915 with troops transported from the western front.

The Allies had to make a swift countermove. England and France could not let the Germans pound Russia to pieces without trying to help.

Winston Churchill, First Lord of the Admiralty, had asked, late in 1914, "Are there not other alternatives than sending our armies to chew barbed wire in Flanders?"

Churchill supplied an answer to his own question by proposing that the Royal Navy force a passage of the Dardanelles, a narrow, winding channel leading to the Sea of Marmara and Constantinople.

Churchill's idea had much merit. If the Dardanelles were penetrated and Constantinople (later renamed Istanbul) put at the mercy of British and French warships, Turkey would be forced to her knees. (The only Turkish ammunition factory was at Constantinople.) In addition, an Allied victory in the Dardanelles might induce such neutral countries as Greece, Bulgaria, Rumania and Italy to enter the war in the Allied camp—the bait to tempt them would be an offer of territorial gains at the expense of Turkey and Austria.

Should this happen, Austria, surrounded by enemies, would be forced to surrender. Not even the Germans could continue to wage war alone, and Churchill's supporters foresaw total victory by mid-1916 if the Dardanelles could be breached.

Admiral Alfred von Tirpitz, the German Minister of the Navy, underlined the importance of the Dardanelles early in 1915 ". . . should the enemy force through to Constantinople, the war will be decided against us."

Despite the tremendous possibilities of the undertaking, few men in high places gave it the proper backing. Lord Horatio Herbert Kitchener, the British War Minister, reluctantly agreed to the project, but remained dubious about its success and assigned only second-rate officers to the planning and preparation of the operation.

Although Winston Churchill was enthusiastic about the scheme, few colleagues in the Admiralty matched his ardor. Originally, Churchill had conceived of an amphibious effort involving troop landings. However, the generals protested they had no men to spare, and Churchill finally agreed that a combined Franco-British naval force of battleships should attempt, by bombardment from the sea, to reduce the forts guarding the Dardanelles. In 1915, the passage was defended by a series of old forts whose guns not only were outranged by the Allied warships but also lacked armor-piercing shells.

The heaviest Turkish cannon were mounted on the Gallipoli Peninsula on the northern flank of the Dardanelles.

In addition to big guns, batteries of howitzers and other field-pieces covered the waterway.

The Turks strewed floating mines in the water and spread antisubmarine nets across the narrowest portion of the strait. These defenses had been supervised by a German, General Liman von Sanders, who revamped the Turkish Army in 1913.

Forcing a way through all this armament was not going to be easy. The first onslaught began February 19, 1915, when eighteen British ships including the *Queen Elizabeth,* whose fifteen-inch guns made her the world's most powerful battleship, opened a bombardment of the Turkish forts. The British were supported by four old French dreadnoughts and numerous tenders, mine sweepers and destroyers. The combined naval force was under the command of Vice Admiral Sackville Carden, a tense and nervous man.

The British and French warships had been pounding away for almost twenty-four hours when a storm forced them to withdraw. The foul weather lasted for nearly a week, and the attack could not be resumed until February 25. It continued, with occasional delays, for about a month.

Even those who had strenuously objected to the Dardanelles operation admitted that Churchill's "scatterbrained" plan seemed likely to succeed. The Turkish forts crumbled under the battering. Gun emplacements were destroyed, and the Turks fled for safety. Parties of daring British blue-jackets and marines went ashore almost at will to destroy with explosives enemy machine-gun posts and other installations.

By March 18, the forts at the entrance to the Dardanelles had been silenced, and the Franco-British flotilla entered the channel. The major obstacle left was a string of twenty mines for which the Turks had no replacements.

The Gallipoli Penninsula

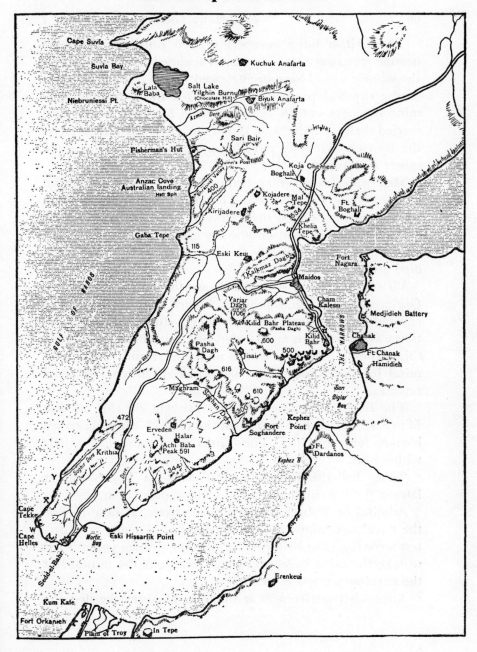

The British mine sweepers probed cautiously into the narrow waterway. Had they been manned by a naval force, the passage would have been cleared without hesitation. Due to the slipshod preparations made for the expedition, the mine sweepers—which were converted fishing trawlers—still carried their civilian crews. When the Turks fired upon them, the trawlers promptly put about, leaving a dozen or more mines still intact.

Meanwhile, devastating shellfire from the ships had all but crushed Turkish resistance. The remaining shore defenses were smashed. Besides, the Turks had used almost all their ammunition; they had only thirty armor-piercing shells left per gun. By 2:00 P.M., Turkish counterfire had practically died away.

Victory pennants fluttered from the mainmast of the *Queen Elizabeth,* and jubilant French and British sailors cheered their apparent triumph. Then, stunningly, the situation was reversed. In rapid order, two British and one French ship struck mines. The vessels went under and English Admiral John de Robeck, who had replaced Carden, signaled a retreat.

The haphazard mine sweeping brought on this setback. March 18, which had started on the crest of triumph, ended bleakly for the Allies. The Turks were astounded at the withdrawal.

"They had the dagger at our throats," a Turkish officer later said. "We could not have fought another hour."

Admiral de Robeck received orders from London to cease the naval operations as "too dangerous." An outraged protest arose from the British sailors. Scores of them volunteered to take the mine sweepers in and clean out the mines. But the naval attack was not renewed.

After hasty conferences at the War Ministry the decision

was made to take the Dardanelles by landing troops on Gallipoli. A 78,000-man British force of the Anzac (Australian and New Zealand) Corps was pulled together.

The Anzacs had to re-equip and load their transports at Alexandria, Egypt. Poor staff work delayed them until April 25, when the commander, General Sir Ian Hamilton, finally brought the troops into position for the landings.

The Anzacs stormed ashore at Cape Helles, which was where the Turks knew they would come, having been so advised by German spies based in Alexandria. General Liman von Sanders had carefully prepared for the invasion—machine guns enfiladed the beaches; artillery batteries were zeroed in.

The Cape Helles landings gained a foothold; that it had been achieved at all was due only to Anzac courage. Other British troops went ashore at various points without meeting any opposition, but General Hamilton issued such vague orders that these units, which could have outflanked the Turks, did not move off the beaches.

One Anzac attack, improvised on the spot, almost captured a key Turkish position. It was beaten back at the last moment by the arrival of Turkish reinforcements under Mustafa Kemal, later to be known as "Ataturk," the Father of Modern Turkey.

The lot of the Anzacs at Cape Helles grew intolerable. The Turks held the heights and kept up a steady, murderous fire on the men below. The wounded suffered agonies; drinking water ran out and it was discovered that all the medical supplies had been misplaced. A search unearthed them in the bottom of a transport's hold, but it took days to unload that precious cargo.

The rocky beach was crowded with men, guns, horses, ammunition and rations. Crates, boxes and bales made an unbelievable clutter. There was no room to maneuver as more troops jammed the teeming beachhead. Seldom in history had a major military operation been so badly mismanaged.

Even worse than Turkish shells and bullets was an outbreak of dysentery caused by a combination of heat, unsanitary conditions, spoiled food and brackish water. Great swarms of flies and insects hovered around the men. Hundreds fell sick. Many died. But the Anzacs clung to their perimeter and kept trying to capture the high ground.

Gallipoli became a synonym for hell. The fighting dragged on for weeks with neither side gaining any decisive advantage. Allied losses mounted, but the Turks suffered heavily, too. They lost almost ten thousand men in one fruitless charge to dislodge the Anzacs.

The campaign brought a mixed blessing for the Allies. Italy, which had maintained an uncertain neutrality, finally decided that Austria was close to collapse and the Turks nearly beaten. On May 23, King Victor Emmanuel's advisers urged him to declare war on Austria so that Italy could put in her claim for the Tyrol and Trieste when Austria surrendered.

Happy people crowded the *piazzas* in Rome and other Italian cities when the annoucement of war was made." *Vive l'Italia!*" the masses shouted. "Long Live Italy!" At last Italy was on the march, not cringing on the side lines; now the world would see how the descendants of the ancient Romans could fight! Bands played, throngs paraded and troop trains rolled northward to attack the despised Austrians.

But Italy's entry into the war scarcely changed the situation at Gallipoli or in the Balkans. Indecisive battles flared along the mountainous Italo-Austrian border in a region described by a correspondent as "a rocky, inaccessible waste-land," and the agony of Gallipoli stretched on.

The British General Staff, which originally had opposed the Gallipoli Campaign, was now compelled to reinforce the troops there. Early in August, the British effected a surprise landing near Suvla Bay, where Turkish forces were deployed thinly. An attack from the new beachheads would have routed the Turks, outflanked the Peninsula's defenses and allowed the long-suffering Anzacs to take the heights. But an incompetent British general commanded at Suvla Bay. Once his troops were ashore, he retired to a destroyer, leaving the men without orders. For two days, the British romped on the beach and did not attack.

General Liman von Sanders, astride his horse on the un-defended heights, looked down at the skylarking enemy. He turned in wonderment to an aide and said, "The sun must have driven them mad! Else why do they not attack?"

When the British finally moved, the opportunity was gone. General von Sanders had rushed men to the heights above Suvla Bay, and the British attack was repulsed.

Gallipoli, which offered so much promise, could end only in disappointment. Turkey was saved and the Dardanelles remained closed.

As a result, Russia was inevitably doomed and brave Serbia left helpless. In September, the Turks, aided by an Austro-German force, overwhelmed that little country. Bulgaria, now emboldened to act against Serbia, entered the war against her, and soon the Serbian Army was in full retreat. After a grueling march across the mountains, the Serbian troops staggered into Allied-held Salonika, which the British and French occupied to keep some hold in the Balkans.

Of greater importance to the British than Serbia was the fate of their 134,000 troops still entrenched on Gallipoli.

The men had to be evacuated under Turkish guns. Starting in December, this phase was carried off with astounding skill and efficiency. Each night men, equipment and animals were withdrawn from Suvla Bay. The Turks did not know what was afoot until the last British soldier was safely away.

The retreating troops had rigged machine guns and rifles to fire by contriving a device which dripped water into tin cans attached to the weapons. When the can was filled with water, its weight pulled the trigger. All night long, machine guns chattered and rifles cracked to keep the Turks cowering in their trenches.

The Suvla Bay evacuation was completed with only one man wounded. The Turks then anticipated the departure from Cape Helles. They were on the alert for that British maneuver. However, the move was also accomplished without hindrance. Under the cover of darkness, units crept out of the line and were carried to waiting ships. By January 9, 1916, only a small rear guard was left.

The enraged Turks, realizing that they had been duped, unloosed a full-scale attack on the remnants of the Anzac garrison. The tiny force tore the Turkish attack to ribbons with a furious concentration of machine-gun fire. Then they, too, were taken to the ships.

The Gallipoli adventure was over. Until the evacuation it had been marked by stupidity, fumbling and incompetence.

"If we'd run the campaign at the beginning the way we did the end of it, you'd see the Union Jack flying over Constantinople," an Anzac officer grumbled.

The nine-month-long operation had been a costly one. Of 489,000 Allied soldiers, 252,000 became casualties. The Turks hardly fared better. They lost 251,309 killed, wounded and missing out of a force that also numbered some 500,000.

Yet, the gamble had been a worthy one. "The Dardanelles

Expedition remains one of history's greatest 'If's.' . . . If only
it had been better handled who knows how many lives
would have been saved in the long run? Who knows if the
world might have been spared the horrors of World War II?
No man can say. He can only wonder," a historian recently
wrote.

2

THE FATEFUL VOYAGE

ON JANUARY 1, 1915, A NEW YORK NEWSPAPER EDITORIAL SAID: "Humanity is weltering in a sea of blood . . . mankind is being wiped out. But we must remain aloof. Let at least one nation survive as a haven of sanity amidst the madness raging elsewhere. . . ."

By 1915, the United States had grown accustomed to existing in a world of war. People became accustomed to the casualties and the ghastly slaughter.

Americans clung hard to normality. They thrilled when the first transcontinental telephone call was completed on January 25, and flocked to movie houses to laugh at the antics of a new comedian, Charlie Chaplin, just rising to fame in a series of short film comedies made by Mack Sennett.

On a day in April when thousands of Russians, Serbs, Britons, Frenchmen, Germans and Austrians were dying on far-flung battlefields, Americans danced in the streets at the news that Jess Willard, a Kansas cowboy, had won the heavyweight championship in Havana, Cuba, from Jack Johnson, a Negro.

"L'il Arthur," as Johnson was called, the first of his race to wear the heavyweight crown, had held the championship seven years. During that time, the American public clamored for a "white hope" to wrest the title from the Negro. Narrow-minded individuals who felt it to be disgraceful that the heavyweight champion was not a white man hailed and toasted Jess Willard as the savior of "Caucasian supremacy."

But neither long-distance telephones, movie comedians nor prizefighters could long divert people's mind from the war. It crept into American lives in many ways. The cost of living began to rise. A quart of milk priced at ten cents in 1914 had jumped to fifteen cents. Before the war beefsteak was twenty-five cents per pound; it now sold for thirty cents. Rents soared higher; coal cost more; clothing, shoes, blankets and bread all became more expensive. Irish linens and British woolens were no longer available. Polish hams and German *wursts* vanished from the shelves.

Across the Atlantic, civilization was being pounded to rubble. The ocean that lapped the eastern coast of the United States was littered with the wreckage and debris of torpedoed ships, for the Germans had resorted to large-scale submarine warfare.

At the outbreak of war, England threw a naval blockade around Germany. Soon, sea-borne traffic to that country was at a standstill. With few exceptions, the Kaiser's ships no longer sailed the seas; nor did neutral vessels put in at German ports.

England's maritime traffic carried on as usual, with ships hauling foodstuffs and munitions from every corner of the British Empire and also the United States. British passenger steamship lines such as Cunard scheduled regular runs between New York, Queenstown, Cobh, Liverpool, Southampton, Plymouth and elsewhere. Travel to and from England was almost normal. Thus, the British Merchant Marine as well as the Royal Navy helped tighten the noose around Germany. The Kaiser had to retaliate in a drastic manner.

On February 10, 1915, the Germans announced that after February 18, all waters around the British Isles would be considered a "war zone." German submarines (U-boats) operating in that area had orders to sink all enemy ships "even if it meant not being always able to save their crews and passengers." According to the Germans, even neutral ships had to run the hazards of naval warfare. "Such vessels cannot be spared from attacks meant for enemy ships." In short, the Germans intended to sink every ship they found in the vicinity of the British Isles.

Americans boiled at this decree. Although British warships had stopped several United States freighters at sea to search for contraband, no one had been hurt. The British menaced no American lives. Now the Germans posed a threat to all ships, including those flying the Stars and Stripes. With submarines lurking like wolves, no person traveling the Atlantic was safe.

President Wilson reacted swiftly to the U-boat warning. He handed Count Johann von Bernstorff, the German ambassador to the United States, a note which stated:

> . . . the U.S. government will hold the Imperial German Government to strict accountability for American lives and shipping lost through submarine action . . . and intends to secure for American citizens the full enjoyment of their rights on the high seas. . . .

These were strong words and the American people, regardless of political differences, backed Wilson all the way. Some even felt he had not gone far enough. A cabinet member, Secretary of Interior Franklin K. Lane, told a friend: "Wilson was too polite, talking Princeton English to a water-front bully."

The German submarine campaign began on schedule. Merchant ships were torpedoed off the coast of Ireland and England with increasing frequency. An American freighter, the *Gulflight,* fell victim to a submarine off the Scilly Islands with a loss of three lives. A week later the Germans sank the Cunard liner *Lusitania,* a 30,395-ton four-stack luxury liner which carried 3,000 passengers and crew. The queen of the Cunard fleet, she was the fastest ship afloat, and had crossed the Atlantic on a record run of four days, four hours and eleven minutes.

A notice inserted by the German Imperial Embassy had appeared in New York newspapers on Friday, April 30. It warned that all ships flying the British flag were in danger of submarine attack and advised travelers sailing on such vessels they were doing so at their own risk.

This announcement ran directly under the Cunard Line's advertisement of the company's shipping schedule for May, which showed the *Lusitania* due to sail at 10:00 A.M. Saturday, May 1, for Liverpool. Despite the German threat not a single passenger canceled his booking.

The *Lusitania* reached the coast of Ireland on Friday, May 7, after a pleasant and uneventful voyage. At 2:00 P.M., her promenade decks were crowded with passengers pointing out landmarks along the coastline. Nobody on the great ship knew that the *Lusitania* was being observed through the periscope of a U-boat submerged about 700 meters away. The submarine, the *U-20,* was commanded by Leutnant-Kapitan Schweiger, who gave an order that was to make war inevitable between the United States and Germany.

At precisely 2:05 P.M. Schweiger snapped, "Fire one torpedo!"

"*Torpedo los!*" came the response. "The torpedo is away!"

The missile leaped from its tube and hurtled through the calm water straight for the *Lusitania's* bow. It struck at 2:08 P.M. and detonated with an explosion that shattered the huge ship.

The ocean queen was mortally wounded. Smoke billowed from her depths, and she started to sink at the bow, where a huge hole had been blown into her hull.

Passengers scurried about her slanting deck. Some leaped into the ocean and were drowned. Others were pitched into the water when overcrowded lifeboats capsized. The liner went under in twenty minutes. The suction caused by the sinking ship dragged hundreds of struggling people to their deaths.

The toll was tremendous. Schweiger's torpedo killed 1,198 men, women and children including 33 babies. Of the 188 Americans aboard the *Lusitania,* 114 died in that disaster.

Revulsion gripped the United States when the wanton torpedoing became known. Newspapers labeled it "deliberate murder." Anti-German feelings rose to a pitch and were fanned by the arrogance with which German officials excused the incident. They claimed the *Lusitania* had been carrying munitions and thus was a suitable target. This charge could not be proved because the ship's manifest had been lost in the sinking, but the allegation was hotly denied by officials of the Cunard Line.

A German spokesman in the United States aroused bitter protests when he stated: "The passengers were warned of an attack. They should have heeded. No one can hold Germany responsible if those foolish people chose to commit suicide."

Leutnant-Kapitan Schweiger became a national hero in his Fatherland. The sinking of the *Lusitania* was commemorated by a special medal, and Schweiger received the Iron Cross, First Class, for his feat. (The "hero" and his submarine did not long survive. In mid-1916, a British destroyer sank the *U-20.*)

Not since 1898 when the battleship *Maine* was blown up

had Americans reacted with the anger they showed over the *Lusitania*. A parallel was drawn between the *Maine* and the *Lusitania*, the destruction of the former had resulted in the Spanish-American War. Many prominent Americans now called for war on Germany.

"The corpses of one hundred and fourteen innocent Americans mutely cry for vengeance!" a congressman ranted. "Shall the cruel murderers of our countrymen go unpunished?"

Ex-President Theodore Roosevelt, who once had favored neutrality, changed his tune. "It is inconceivable that we should refrain from action! We must act! We owe it to ourselves and to humanity."

The American people turned to President Wilson in this terrible moment. He had promised that Germany would be held to "strict accountability" for American lives. Surely, Mr. Wilson would show the world that no "goose-stepping Hun" could kill Americans and get away with it!

Americans waited eagerly for the President to speak about the *Lusitania*. His first words on the subject were startling: "There is such a thing as a nation being so right that it does not need to convince others by force that it is right. . . . There is such a thing as being *too proud to fight!*"

Wilson's remarks aroused a storm over the nation. Hotheads called him a coward, but calmer men saw the wisdom in Wilson's forbearance. The United States was not prepared for war. In 1915, the American Army numbered less than 100,000 men; the Navy, "the first line of defense," was far understrength in ships and personnel. Logically, the United States should settle the *Lusitania* affair by diplomacy if possible and resort to force only if every other means failed.

Diplomatic exchanges passed between the Germans and the United States for nearly a year. Finally, Wilson lost patience. He called in von Bernstorff and sternly told him that unless Germany stopped sinking unarmed passenger ships, the United States would sever diplomatic relations.

The German government bowed to Wilson by agreeing that their U-boat captains would "refrain from sinking merchant ships without warning and without saving human lives."

The Germans followed this course because, by 1916, the Allies had found effective antisubmarine tactics. Merchant ships traveled in convoys shepherded by fast destroyers. Flying boats, dirigibles and speedy motor boats called "subchasers" had dispatched many submarines. Radio-operated listening devices to detect U-boats from a distance were being developed, and for the moment, the Germans felt it wise to make some concessions.

They had many new U-boats on the ways in their shipyards—a huge fleet of submarines that would be ready for action by early 1917. The Germans did not want to lose trained sub captains and crews before these additional U-boats were completed.

Wilson was mollified by his diplomatic victory, and from May 4, 1916, until January 31, 1917, U-boat attacks fell off sharply.

However, on January 31, 1917, the Germans renewed unrestricted submarine attacks. It was a reign of fright at sea never before equaled. Submarines roved the Atlantic in two's and three's like "wolf packs" to ring a cordon of death about the British Isles. The captains had orders to "sink without a trace" any vessel approaching England, regardless of flag or markings.

Even hospital ships and food ships flying the flag of the International Red Cross were made targets. Thousands of lives and scores of merchantmen were lost during the brutal period of U-boat terror.

"We lulled the Allies into believing our submarine weapon had been laid aside," a German official gloated. "Let it be recorded that we never intended to fight a so-called gentleman's war with our U-boats. Terror, terror and more terror was always our slogan. In 1916, the lull in our submarine activity was merely a breathing spell, as the world soon learned. . . ."

3

"SOME SCARRED SLOPE . . ."

SPRING CAME TO EUROPE AND GREEN SHOOTS INCONGRUOUSLY
poked out of the tortured, battle-ravaged earth. But in 1915,
spring brought no promise except of death and suffering. A
young American poet, Alan Seeger, fighting as a volunteer in
the French Foreign Legion, reflected the feelings of his con-
temporaries by writing:

> I have a rendezvous with Death
> On Some scarred slope of battered hill,
> When Spring comes round again this year
> And the first meadow flowers appear.

Thousands upon thousands of youths kept that rendezvous.
The Allied generals had spent the winter trying to find some
strategy to crack the enemy lines in the West. More than two
million Germans manned trenches that ran in an irregular
line from Switzerland to the English Channel. In the trenches
opposite were about three million French and British soldiers.

Papa Joffre and the French high command still clung to
the theory of the attack despite the terrible losses of 1914.
"We will yet skewer the *boches* on our bayonets," one of
Joffre's staff officers boasted. The fact that a soldier had to
come within a few feet of the enemy to "skewer" him on a

bayonet apparently escaped him. The French generals seemed unable to comprehend that frontal assault could only mean slaughter for the attackers. Joffre refused to acknowledge that the old ways of making war had passed and the times called for new techniques and tactics.

The British commander, General Sir John French, was scarcely better. He still spoke of mass attacks to "smash the enemy's lines," and the men of the B.E.F. died valiantly to prove him wrong. His successor, General Sir Douglas Haig, was a former cavalryman trained to swift forays and slashing assaults. He, too, believed the way to beat the Germans was by overwhelming frontal attacks. Haig, like French, Joffre and others, had not learned to fight a twentieth-century war.

Less hidebound than the Allies and more willing to experiment with new weapons and strategy, the German General Staff also threw men away in futile attacks.

The war in the West was a grisly slugging match. Soldiers died in droves to win a few yards of muddy earth. For the Allies it became a struggle of attrition based on the cold-blooded assumption that the side with a few men still alive when all the enemy were dead would be the victor.

Even before spring set in, while the ground was frozen solid and the snows unmelted, the French attacked on February 15, in the Champagne area between Rheims and Massiges. The objective of the assault was a German railroad supply line five miles to the rear. After a month the French could show gains of less than a quarter-mile, for which thousands of men died. The German casualties, though heavy, were far less than the French losses.

The British attacked near Noyon on March 10 and, for the first time in the war, used large-scale aerial reconnaissance. In 1915, cameras for aircraft had been perfected and proved invaluable to intelligence officers for spotting supply dumps, troop concentrations, artillery batteries and other military objectives.

As yet, no planes suitable for bombing had been developed; but they would soon be in the air, along with swift fighter craft, so that for the first time in the ugly history of war, men would battle in the skies.

The British attack in the Noyon sector opened on schedule with a violent artillery barrage. Bayonet-wielding infantry followed across No Man's Land. The British were confident no Germans could survive the bombardment. But the enemy ducked into his deep dugouts until the shelling ended and then mowed down the advancing Tommies with machine guns.

The attack stalled dead in three hours after moving forward less than a mile. This trivial gain cost the British 3,266 men an hour. This was the ghastly toll of war. And while the hordes of crippled, blinded and shattered men stumbled home from the trenches, generals blustered about a "breakthrough" and politicians made flowery speeches larded with the promise of victory.

But in Berlin and Paris, in London, Petrograd and Rome, in the cities and the devastated lands of Belgium and France, in the mountain passes of Serbia and Montenegro, in the wild reaches of the Carpathians and the broad plains of Hungary, the ordinary people mourned their dead sons and the monstrous war ground on.

Obviously, some means to end the deadlock in the West had to be found. The Germans were the first to use a cruel weapon with the potential of winning the war.

On April 22, a splendid spring day throbbing with sunshine, the long-dormant Ypres sector burst into flaming life under a German barrage. At 5:00 P.M., as the sun was about to set, a yellow-green mist carried by the breeze, rolled toward the Allied trenches. It was highly poisonous chlorine gas that the Germans had released from more than five thousand cylinders.

The deadly cloud descended upon the trenches of a French regiment, and the men who breathed those noxious fumes stumbled away, choking, retching, gasping for air. Panic spread among the afflicted troops, and they fled, leaving a gap in the lines.

However, the Germans dared not exploit the opening; they also feared the gas, and the support troops which were to have rushed in hesitated until darkness. The opportunity was lost. The next morning, British troops plugged the gap. Poison gas, now an established weapon, was used again in the battle, but without effect.

The Allies also had chlorine gas by September, a season when the prevailing winds were westerly in the direction of the German lines. Then Germans fell under the death-dealing fog.

Soon, respirators (gas masks) were issued to the troops. Poison gas never became a decisive factor, although types deadlier than chlorine were produced. Before the war ended, German chemists added "mustard gas" to their arsenal of horror. This chemical not only choked a victim but also left ghastly blisters on his skin.

The British and French continued to mount abortive attacks throughout 1915. On one front, Papa Joffre ordered a three-day bombardment with 2,500 guns of German lines. For seventy-two hours high explosives raked the German positions. Joffre sent horse cavalry with the great attack that followed when the guns finally fell silent. That barrage, he thought, must batter the German defenders into submission. But when the cannon stopped, the enemy again crept out of his holes and decimated the French infantry and cavalry with automatic weapons.

The British fared little better in an offensive launched around Artois. A dawn assault on October 14 was preceded by clouds of poison gas which literally blanketed the German trenches. At first the Kaiser's troops fell back, especially in the mining region near Loos. They soon rallied, however, and once again the machine guns did their work. When the fighting ended after three days the British counted 60,000 casualties; the Germans about 20,000.

This battle toppled Sir John French from his post as commander-in-chief of the three British armies in France. At year's end, he was replaced by General Sir Douglas Haig, a fifty-four-year-old Scotsman, who had achieved a fine record in the army during his lifelong career. Haig, although wealthy, was a professional soldier of many years' service.

The troops Haig commanded were vastly different from those that had gone to France and Belgium in August, 1914. Throughout 1915, the Army had been filled by volunteers, but after January, 1916, the British government resorted to conscription for the first time in history.

Thus, the British Army, which had once been a professional elite, now represented a cross section of the nation. Yorkshire farmers and Oxford graduates marched shoulder to shoulder. London socialites and Welsh coal miners learned to drill, march and fight.

The war was bringing a social revolution to England. No one stormed barricades or raised the red flag; but a revolution was taking place. The rigid class system cracked under the war's stress. A muddy, battle-weary soldier, sharing a rain-filled dugout in a Flanders trench, did not bother about the backgrounds of his trenchmates. When the enemy shells started falling, it mattered little that a man could trace his lineage to William the Conqueror and was listed in the social register.

"The German Maxim machine gun and eighty-eight millimeter cannon are the two greatest equalizers since the dawn of civilization," an English officer said. "We have learned that every man is the same in the trenches."

The average Briton soon demonstrated that he made a good soldier—to the dismay of the Germans, who kept insisting that the "nation of shopkeepers" had no stomach for real fighting.

England and all Europe had learned by 1915 that this war was different from any other fought. In the past, noncombatant civilians were sometimes swept up in the tide of war—cities had been sacked, women and children killed by invading armies, atrocities committed. That was the nature of war. But then civilians caught in the fighting were in the path of the armies, not hundreds of miles behind the lines.

During January, 1915, another face was added to modern warfare. Shortly after New Year's Day, German Zeppelins (hydrogen-filled rigid airships driven by engines) bombed the English coast. Soon, there were attacks by Zeppelins on both Paris and London. The Era of Total War had begun: there was no longer a front line; with the advent of air power, still an infant in 1915, no one was safe from the dangers of war. Airplanes, poison gases, submarines and long-range cannon made war a universal horror no longer limited to the battlefield.

The Allies threw men into the crucible until 1,500,000 had become casualties in the West. The Germans also paid a high price for holding their lines in Belgium and France: 600,000 of the Kaiser's soldiers spilled their blood for the Fatherland in 1915.

On the eastern front, the year proved a disastrous one for Tsar Nicholas. Two million Russian were killed, wounded or missing during a series of battles which ended with deep German advances into the Russian heartland. At least 1,000,-000 Russians were taken prisoner in these military debacles.

The Eastern Battle Front

Despite the reverses, the Tsar's troops had inflicted heavy losses on Germany's ally, Austria, and, for a time, threatened an invasion of Hungary through the Carpathian Mountain passes. But the Germans came to the rescue and forced the Russians to go onto the defensive all along the line.

Back, and back again, reeled the Russian armies. To fill the gaps in the ranks, recruits with but a month's training were rushed into the lines. Many of them carried no weapon but a club. "Pick up a dead man's rifle on the battlefield," officers told them.

It seemed incredible that Russia could carry on the war much longer. But the Dark People heeded the Little Father on the throne in Petrograd (formerly St. Petersburg). The masses died willingly for their Tsar; in 1915, he was still an unsullied symbol chosen to rule Holy Mother Russia by divine power. The Dark People could not yet see the corruption, the avarice and greed of the Russian ruling class as represented by the Tsar. The Russians had not suffered enough to rise up against their Tsar. But beneath the surface were the warning rumblings of an earthquake in the making.

None in the Russian ruling class heeded the distant thunder, least of all the Tsar. He kept on in the old autocratic manner, refusing to liberalize his government, rejecting all proposals to ease the want among his people. Bread lines were forming in Petrograd. Children went barefoot, for shoes cost too much. Families shivered in the Russian cold without fires because they had no coal. The Germans had seized the Ukraine, which was Russia's breadbasket. Hunger, want and privation stalked the country; in a land where need was common and bread a luxury, thousands perished of starvation. But the Russians still clutched their mystic concept of Tsar and Holy Russia; when the Little Father called, they went forth to battle.

General August von Mackensen, who commanded a German army in Russia, confidently declared: "The Russian will to resist is broken. Her power is smashed. The end is at hand. I predict we shall celebrate Christmas in Petrograd!"

Von Mackensen's prophecy went unfulfilled. Many thousands of Germans were to find graves in Russian soil before the war in the East ended.

Dire events were being readied, happenings that were to change Russia and affect the entire world. But in 1915 no man had the prescience to foretell what was coming. While his people grew pinched, the Tsar lived in lavish splendor. The courtiers scraped and bowed before him and the monk Rasputin held the royal family in his evil grip.

In Russia those who should have listened were deaf to whispers of discontent. And because they did not listen, the whispers would rise to a shout and the discontent transform itself into a revolution which would shake centuries-old social structures and economic systems, topple monarchies and spread the class struggle over the face of the earth.

4

MR. FORD'S "ARK OF PEACE"

AS THE WAR DRAGGED INTO ITS SECOND YEAR, MANY PEOPLE IN the neutral nations, especially the United States, wondered if some way could be found to end the carnage by arbitration. The sinking of the *Lusitania* had snapped most Americans out of their lethargy toward the war. The German U-boat campaign put the conflict on America's doorstep.

Some Americans were violently pro-Allied while others backed the Kaiser. Some groups wanted to fight Germany; some demanded absolute neutrality, while at least one Irish society called for war against England and the seizure of Canada.

Foreign language papers bloomed on every hand. Each urged its adopted country to back one side or the other. The dissension among Americans of foreign extraction created serious unpleasantnesses.

Old World hatreds were rekindled. This gave an opportunity for reactionary native-born Americans to launch vicious attacks against their foreign-born countrymen. Congress was bombarded with demands to restrict future immigration "as a safeguard for our way of life."

Controversies raged up and down the country. As differences grew sharper, persons of similar racial and national background banded together. For the first time in the nation's history the term "hyphenated American" was used. People spoke of themselves as Polish-Americans, German-Americans, Italian-Americans, Russian-Americans and all the polyglot groupings that made up the Austro-Hungarian Empire.

Ex-President Theodore Roosevelt thundered: "There is no such thing as a hyphenated American! A citizen of this country is either one hundred per cent American or he is nothing!"

While invective and divided loyalties shook the nation, Americans were even further torn between those who believed in keeping the United States out of war by building up the Army and the Navy and those opposed to that idea.

"An Army of a million and a Navy second to none! We must be prepared! Uncle Sam must show his muscle!" the preparedness backers urged.

Contrary to this view stood the pacifists. Some sought to keep the United States out of the present war and denounced all military preparation as jingoistic warmongering. Their peace-loving motives were suspect since they adopted the policies and propaganda of pro-German elements.

Many sincere pacifists in America spoke out against all war. Their slogan was: "The only way to keep America out of war is to keep war out of the world!" The pacifists were targets of ridicule especially from exponents of preparedness. "Yellow bellies," "milksops" and "cowards" were among the milder epithets hurled at the pacifists, who retaliated by calling their detractors "bloody-handed militarists" and similar terms. Often, the language exchanged between the two groups was neither that scholary nor polite; sometimes brickbats, fists and rocks took the place of words.

A Tin Pan Alley songwriter gave the pacifist movement a theme song when he wrote a popular tune, "I Didn't Raise My Boy To Be A Soldier."

The most spectacular effort by American pacifists occurred during the closing months of 1915 when Hungarian-born Rosa Schwimmer, a delegate to the International Women's Peace Conference at The Hague, was touring the United States delivering talks on achieving peace through mediation.

Mrs. Schwimmer's receptions in the cities she visited ranged from cool to lukewarm and failed to gain mass support for her worthy cause. In early November Mrs. Schwimmer came to Detroit, where she learned from a newspaper, *The Detroit Free Press,* that Henry Ford, the auto magnate, had stated: "This stupid war's been going on long enough. I'd give half my fortune to shorten it by even a single day!"

Earnest Mrs. Schwimmer was delighted; here was an influential convert to the side of peace. She decided to see Ford and have a talk with him. But this was not so easily accomplished. The automobile manufacturer was guarded by a host of secretaries and underlings who shunted her from one to the other.

A person less determined than she would have given up; but the pacifist lady was a stubborn soul. After many discouragements, she finally reached Ford and outlined to him her hopes for ending the war through mediation.

Ford liked the plan so much that he decided, on the spot, to back it. "I'll do more than give you my support," he promised Mrs. Schwimmer. "I'll go to Europe myself and take a hand in the negotiations. It's my opinion that the fighting nations are sick of war. They want to stop and are only waiting for some disinterested party to step in and offer a way out. I may be that party."

Ford was sincere in his desire to do something about the war. Ever since its outbreak he had expressed disgust over the conflict's "moral wrongs." His decision to help Mrs. Schwimmer and go to Europe was no grandstand play; millions of ordinary Americans shared his impulse. They also wanted to do something about ending the war but lacked both the means and the influence to do it.

Henry Ford, however, had fame, prestige and wealth; he had access to the highest officials of the warring powers. His chances for success as a peacemaker were good. Unlike professional diplomats, he was not bound by protocol. A topnotch salesman, the King of Detroit could speak frankly to the kings of Europe and might well persuade them to end the bloodshed. Ford was confident that he could carry off the mission.

"All they need over there is someone to talk good, common horse sense, that's all," he said. "I'll get to the core of the trouble and then root it out. There must be some better solution to world problems than war. Anything's better than the savagery of war. War is a reversion to the days of the cave man. We can tolerate it no longer!"

Within the week, Ford moved to New York, rented a suite of rooms at the Hotel Biltmore and offered his services to a pacifist group organized by Mrs. Schwimmer. It had headquarters at the Hotel McAlpin for which the industrialist footed the bill.

Ford soon had sparks flying. He chartered a Scandinavian Line ship, the *Oscar II*, to carry the peace delegates to Europe. The ship was scheduled to depart on December 4. Although much had to be done in less than two weeks, Ford's energy and money overcame most of the problems.

He mobilized a corps of stenographers and typists to handle the correspondence for the "Peace Pilgrimage." Hundreds of invitations to sail aboard the *Oscar II* were sent out. Every congressman and senator, all governors, the mayors of large cities, university presidents, educators, doctors, lawyers, engineers, journalists and other notables were included in the list.

To Ford's amazement, few invitations were readily accepted. William Jennings Bryan begged off the voyage by claiming he "could do more good for peace at home." President Wilson's daughter, Margaret, an outspoken peace advocate, also declined. Most senators and congressmen refused to make the junket, and the only governor to take up the bid was an open militarist who announced he was only going over "to see the war."

Ford's reaction was: "I guess they find talking against war lots easier than doing something about it." He went to Washington and visited President Wilson, hoping to get his official sanction for the trip. When the President failed to back the voyage, King Henry stalked angrily out of the White House.

Far more damaging than this presidential rebuff was the press-inspired reaction of the general public. The newspapers ridiculed the mission, and the public laughed in derision. No one was sure why a peace effort should become a target for mockery, but the *Oscar II* was torpedoed by mass opinion before she sailed.

A remark by one of Ford's aides had loosed the flood of journalistic sarcasm. "It is our purpose to get the boys out of the trenches by Christmas!" a press representative told a news conference on December 1.

After that the peace ship never had a chance. "What miracle workers these pacifists are! They'll have the boys out of the trenches by Christmas! Why, we'll barely have our holiday shopping done!" a columnist sneered.

The phrase "out of the trenches by Christmas!" became a standing joke. Any music hall comic could break up his audience by using it. Anything from a new hat to a politician's speech could be ridiculed as being "out of the trenches by Christmas!" In the slang of that day, the peace ship was a "scream."

Almost swamped by the tidal wave of mockery, Ford and his followers worked against mounting difficulties. His suite at the Biltmore was deluged with "cranks, crackpots, fanatics, opportunists, con men and looneys who wanted to go along for the ride," a newsman recalled.

There were also people of purpose and importance in that motley crowd, but the press ignored the solid citizens and played up the antics of the "inmates of Ford's lunatic asylum."

The peace ship was rebuffed abroad as well as at home. Norway was the only nation to offer the delegates hospitality. The other countries, belligerents and neutrals alike, treated the mission with disdain.

Nevertheless, the *Oscar II* sailed from Hoboken, New Jersey, on December 4, 1915, at 3:00 P.M. Aboard were fifty-four newspaper and magazine correspondents, three movie newsreel cameramen, Ford's personal staff of twenty and some sixty delegates.

The departure of "Mr. Ford's Ark of Peace," as *The New York Sun* labeled the ship, was a carnival, with blaring bands, streamers, confetti, shouts, screams and yells. A huge crowd thronged the pier, and heads were cracked by club-wielding policemen when groups of onlookers started a brawl. The spectators cheered wildly as Thomas Alva Edison went up the gangplank followed by Henry Ford. Cameras clicked, flash powder exploded, whistles tooted. At last, the *Oscar II* was on her way.

When she pulled out, a man leaped off the pier and swam after the ship. A police launch hauled him from the water. "Why did you do it?" asked one of his rescuers.

"I wanted my picture in the paper," the dripping swimmer grinned.

Unfortunately, the "Ark of Peace" failed to accomplish any useful purpose. On Sunday, December 19, 1915, the

Oscar II docked at Christiana, Norway. Ford was quoted as saying, "The landing of the peace pilgrims will be recorded as the most benevolent thing America ever did."

The Norwegians feted the delegates. There were banquets and parties, speeches and praise; but on the winter-locked Continent guns still belched, machine guns hammered, and men died in the frozen wastes of no man's land.

On Christmas Day, when the boys were to have been "out of the trenches," Henry Ford left Norway for home, his "Peace Pilgrimage" buried by an avalanche of international derision.

Safely back in Detroit, Ford held a press conference. "What did you get out of your trip?" a reporter asked.

Ford looked at him quizzically. "It's a cinch I didn't get peace. But I'm a businessman and never miss an opportunity. I landed a big order for farm tractors from the Russians."

The peace ship fiasco was soon forgotten, and the war ran endlessly on. A world surfeited by bloodshed seemed powerless to end the havoc.

"We are trapped in the madness of killing and hate. This is the dance of death and one need not be a prophet to see that we are all doomed," a young English soldier wrote from the trenches of Flanders as 1915 ended.

5

"THEY SHALL NOT PASS!"

THE FUROR AROUSED BY HENRY FORD'S WELL-INTENTIONED peace efforts scarcely caused a ripple on the western front, where the contending armies glowered at each other along a thousand miles of trenches.

Both sides prepared for major moves in 1916. Papa Joffre presided over a meeting of Allied military leaders—French, British, Belgian, Russian, Italian and even Japanese officers attended the conference. This would be the year of decision, they decided, and agreed to launch simultaneous massive offensives on the eastern, western and Italian fronts which would "crush the Central Powers like a walnut."

Soon, staff officers were busy studying maps for the best point to hit the enemy. But as the Allies pondered their strategy, the German commander in the West, General Erich von Falkenhayn, beat them to the punch. He had a positive theory for winning trench warfare. Von Falkenhayn wrote:

> A breakthrough is almost impossible in this day of the machine gun . . . to attain victory one should pick a sector of attack, for the retention of which the enemy must throw in every man he has. . . . Once he does this it is then only necessary to hold the foe there and bleed him white.

The time had come for von Falkenhayn to test his idea. During 1915 the Central Powers had won great victories against the Russians and smashed every Allied offensive in the

West. At first glance, it seemed that Germany and her partners were winning the war.

But the military triumphs hid defects in the tapestry. The Allied blockade was growing more effective daily. Inside Germany shortages of food and clothing mounted. Strict rationing was in force and the word *ersatz* (synthetic) was heard more often, as chemists found substitutes for leather, rubber, cotton, wool and hundreds of other products cut off by the blockade. Bakeries turned out *ersatz* bread made with artificial flour. Powdered chicory replaced coffee. Herbs, roots and plants were boiled for soup, and German housewives prepared meals of *ersatz* eggs and *ersatz* sausages. In the beer halls, men drank *ersatz* beer and filled their pipes with *ersatz* tobacco.

The cost of living in Germany zoomed every week; coal was both scarce and costly. The winter had been a severe one. Many people were stricken with colds or the grippe. Medicines were hard to come by on the home front and many civilians had died for lack of medical care.

Conditions in the Austrian Empire also had deteriorated. Franz Josef's domain was cracking up. The tremendous loss of men in Russia, the indecisive struggle against the Italians and the worsening economic situation at home clearly underlined the aged Emperor's troubles.

Most serious was the growing disaffection in the Austro-Hungarian Army. Czech regiments had become mutinous. Units made up of other minorities were restive. If the Germans hoped to keep their Austro-Hungarian allies in the war, something had to be done at once.

General von Falkenhayn proposed to the German high command a plan which he believed would cripple France and bring victory in the West. He suggested a tremendous concentration against the salient at Verdun, where the enemy lines jutted forward so that it could be attacked on three sides.

There (at Verdun) the general proposed to mass more artillery than had ever been used in modern warfare. The guns would range from 12-inch naval cannon to 420-mm. mortars. Monstrous bombardments were to pound the French lines until defenses and defenders had been battered to dust.

According to von Falkenhayn, "The artillery will take the positions for us. . . . Our infantry will only have to advance and occupy it."

He based his approach on the successes the Germans had attained with their siege guns against the Belgian forts at Liege, Maubeuge and Namur in 1914. Those same caliber guns had also battered Russian forts into submission. If they had worked against other fortifications, why not at Verdun?

Von Falkenhayn knew that no matter how severely Verdun was pulverized, the French had to keep defending the ancient fortress city because a withdrawal from it would be a confession that France had lost the war.

The German commander hoped to prolong the battle indefinitely. "Let it last weeks or months . . . the longer the better. As it drags on we will grind up more and more Frenchmen," he said.

After some discussion, the German high command agreed that Verdun was a suitable objective. During the latter part of January, 1916, orders went out to concentrate guns, ammunition and men for the assault on the key French stronghold.

A novel situation had developed in the Verdun sector, dormant since 1914. French military leaders, including Papa Joffre, decided that forts such as those guarding Verdun could not be held. They drew this conclusion from the 1914 fate of the Belgian and Russian bastions.

No one seemed to realize that the Verdun defenses were far better built and armed than either the Belgian or the Russian strongholds. Besides, Verdun's forts had deep under-

The Verdun Area

To Metz

To Vigneulles

Bury

W O E V R E

Fresnes

To Metz

Etain

To Vigneulles

St. Rémy

Combres

Les Éparges

R. Orne

Forest of Spincourt

Moranville

Woods

Manheulles

Haudiomont

Ronvaux

Châtillon

Blanzée

Abaucourt

Mouilly

en-Woëvre

Azannes

Ruins of Ornes

Dieppe

Fromezey

Eix

Damloup

Moulainville Ft.

Moulainville

Belrupt Rozellier Ft

Sommedieue

Rupt

The Meuse

Heights

Bezonvaux

Ornes

Beaumont

Louvemont

B. d'Haudromont

Douaumont Fort

B. d'Hardaumont

Vaux Fort

Tavannes

Ft.

B. des Caillettes

Fleury

Froide Terre

Thiaumont Rdt.

Ft. St. Michel

Souville Ft.

Belleville Ft.

Bras

Charny

Belrupt Ft

Haudainville

Dieue

Fort

Génicourt Ft.

Génicourt

To St. Mihiel

Consenvoye

Brabant-sur-Meuse

Haumont

Samogneux

Régneville

Champneuville

Vacherauville

Marre Ft.

VERDUN

Belleray

Dugny Ft.

Dugny

Ancemont

B. de Forges

Forges

Crow's Wood

Cumières

Chattancourt

R. Meuse

Courra (or. Bourrus) Ft.

Choisel Ft.

Ft. de la Chaume

Landrecourt Ft.

Landrecourt

Lempire

Senoncourt

Sartelles Ft.

Bois de Montfaucon

Bethincourt

Malancourt

Haucourt

B. de Malancourt

B. d'Avocourt

Avocourt

Esnes

Montzéville

Sivry

Jouy

Dombasle

Brabant-en-Argonne

Rampont

Jubécourt

Souhesme

Ville-sur-Couzances

R. Couzances

Vadelaincourt

Lemmes

Railway to Bar-le-Duc

Ippécourt

To Clermont

Recicourt

R. Aire

Froides

Rarécourt

10 Miles

5

0

ground connecting passages which could withstand shellfire even of the heaviest caliber. The forts radiated from Verdun in concentric circles; their machine-gun posts and fields of fire were interlocking. Each strongpoint had been well stocked with food, water and ammunition. The garrisons could hold out indefinitely. In 1916 no artillery shell had the explosive power to smash the forts' thick steel and concrete walls. No infantry attack could have survived the tremendous firepower of the great strongholds.

But the French General Staff decided that the forts were obsolete, and Joffre ordered them stripped of their guns and abandoned. Several were slated for demolition. At the start of 1916, the French defenses around Verdun consisted of dugouts, trenches, bunkers, machine-gun emplacements, barbed wire and other field fortifications adapted to the difficult terrain that followed the Meuse River.

In some places the trench system was quite strong, but its greatest portion had been neglected in the year and a half that the sector had been quiet. As a result, French soldiers, who could have remained in perfect safety behind the protection of the forts, were now exposed to the German guns.

For some undetermined reason, Papa Joffre refused to heed warnings by his intelligence officers that the enemy was mobilizing for an attack on Verdun. Joffre, busy with plans for his own offensive, shrugged off the reports. The Germans, he believed, were using their massive preparations around Verdun as a cover-up for an attack in another sector.

"Otherwise," Papa Joffre said, "the *boches* would not be so obvious."

However, he reinforced the troops around Verdun with two additional divisions and then returned to his maps and the proposed big offensive which was to sweep the Germans out of France.

The Germans had scheduled the Verdun assault to start at dawn, February 12. But a period of cold, rainy weather set in, and visibility was so poor that German artillery observers could not see their targets. The rain also grounded all planes. Since German aircraft, particularly the Fokker D7, then controlled the skies, von Falkenhayn decided to wait until the weather cleared so he could have the benefits of aerial reconnaissance.

It took nine days for the sun to return. On February 21, a bright, cold winter's morning, the German barrage started. The German guns fired two million shells that day from dawn to dusk. It was the greatest bombardment in the history of warfare.

At dusk, German infantry went forward. "You won't find anything alive out there, boys!" a company commander shouted to his men as he led them toward the French trenches. A moment later, he fell, riddled by machine-gun bullets.

All along the thirty-five-mile front, the Germans met stout resistance. Somehow, the *poilus* (a nickname for the ordinary French soldier) had managed to endure the awful shelling. They checked the Germans with rifles at some points and routed them at others.

Specially trained elite German troops equipped with *flammenwerferen* (flame throwers) were called on to drive the French from their bunkers and dugouts. The *poilus* fought as they never had before, in many cases to the last man and the last bullet. They were forced back foot by foot, but made the Germans pay dearly for every inch.

Von Falkenhayn's men kept pushing ahead until February 25. They seized Fort Douaumont, a key point in the Verdun defense. The strongpoint had been abandoned, and the Germans took it without firing a shot or losing a man. It was to take the French eight months and many lives to recapture

Fort Douaumont. Even after they had blasted it with 120,000 shells, they found the interior undamaged and the guns still working.

After Douaumont fell, Joffre issued an order. "Any commander who under the circumstances gives orders to retreat will be court-martialed." He also rushed troops to reoccupy the forts they should have been defending in the first place. This was accomplished just in time.

The defense of Verdun now centered about the forts, and a battle unlike any before raged for months. The struggle for Verdum was an epic of human endurance. The defense of the sector was turned over to General Henri Pétain, who won his glory at Verdun and lost it by dealing with the Germans twenty-four years later, during the Second World War.

Pétain recognized that his major problem was to supply the troops in Verdun. He organized long convoys of motor trucks which rolled day and night into the embattled town along the one usable road. The trucks, loaded with ammunition, rations, medical supplies and other necessities, followed each other at fourteen-second intervals on what became known as *La Voie Sacrée* (the Sacred Way).

The Sacred Way supplied Verdun; but the courage and self-sacrifice of the *poilus* held off the Germans. There were innumerable battles. Such places as *Mort Homme Hill,* (Dead Man's Hill), Hill 304, Fort Vaux and Fort Douaumont became household words. Attacks, counterattacks, hand-to-hand combat, bayonet charges, artillery barrages and counterbarrages shattered the earth and butchered the men fighting at Verdun.

The German Fifth Army commanded by the Kaiser's son, the Crown Prince of Prussia, did most of the fighting for the invader. All through March and April in mud, rain, fog and spring sunshine, the Crown Prince drove his troops forward. But the French held back every German onslaught. All France was electrified by the old battle cry of the Marne *"Ils ne passeront pas!"* (They shall not pass!)

At last, in mid-summer, the Germans seemed to be weakening and Pétain gave the French a new slogan *"On les aura!"* (We'll get them!) as the tide of battle slowly turned in favor of the French. During August, two of Pétain's subordinates, General Robert Nivelle and General Charles Mangin, started a series of counterattacks which ended with the recapture of Fort Douaumont and also Fort Vaux, which had fallen to the Germans in June. The Crown Prince and von Falkenhayn at last realized they could expend no more men. Von Falkenhayn's theory had been proven nearly correct: the French had been bled white—Verdun cost them 315,000 casualties; but the Germans also had spilled rivers of blood, their losses numbering almost 300,000.

At Verdun, both sides fired a total of 23,000,000 high-explosive shells. The best troops of each army fell there. Some historians claim the French never completely recovered from the battle.

An outstanding feature of the struggle was the defeat of the German air force over Verdun. The Fokker D7, which had been the best plane flying at the start of 1916, was driven from the blue by the French Nieuport Pursuit plane and the British Sopwith camel.

Like the Marne, Verdun marked another turning point in the war. For General von Falkenhayn it brought military obscurity; he was relieved in August to be succeeded by Generals Hindenburg and Ludendorff, the victors in the East.

6

THE ARMORED MONSTER

As Frenchmen and Germans were slaughtering each other at Verdun, the focus of attention swung briefly away from that furious hell to center on the long-awaited clash between the British Grand Fleet and the German High Seas Fleet.

The German fleet had a new commander, Admiral Reinhard Scheer, a driving, dynamic officer who vowed he would "break Britain's back" by destroying her navy.

Scheer's aim was to force a showdown battle with the British Grand Fleet. Admiral Sir John Jellicoe, the Royal Navy's chief, also wanted a full-scale fight.

Late in May, 1916, Scheer ordered the High Seas Fleet into action. The German armada sortied out of home waters to the North Sea. Its progress was reported by British naval intelligence, and Jellicoe went into action. The sea battle of the century was shaping up. On May 31, the opposing cruisers met in the North Sea off Jutland, Denmark, near the Skagerrak Strait. A desperate clash started at 3:28 P.M. in the dull overcast of the waning afternoon.

By 4:00 P.M. several British ships had been damaged. Admiral Sir David Beatty, commanding the Royal Navy's cruisers from the bridge of his flagship, H.M.S. *Lion,* which had been struck four times, said to an officer: "The Germans are shooting well today! I'm closing in a bit."

Big guns roared. Men and ships died. Much was at stake

in the Battle of Jutland (which the Germans called the Battle of the Skagerrak). If the Germans won they could break the British blockade and gain supremacy at sea. Scheer fought furiously. He sent his ships against the enemy with a single order: "Victory or death!"

Jellicoe was keenly aware of his responsibilities. "I could not leave anything to chance, because our fleet was the one and only factor vital to the existence of the Empire," he said later. "I could lose the war in a single afternoon. It was a terrible weight to carry."

When the battle ended after dark, three British battle cruisers, three armored cruisers and eight destroyers were at the bottom of the North Sea. The Germans lost one battle cruiser, an old battleship, four light cruisers and five destroyers. Scheer's casualties totaled about three thousand killed, wounded and missing while the British losses numbered almost six thousand.

On paper, the battle was a German triumph, but Jutland actually concluded without any decision. Scheer broke off the engagement, and his ships limped to their bases leaving the wounded British lion still in command of the seas.

Although Germany's naval might had not been smashed at Jutland, the Kaiser's fleet ceased to be any further threat. After the great naval engagement Scheer's squadrons rode at anchor for the remainder of the war; having failed to win total victory, the Germans never again risked a large-scale surface battle, preferring instead to rely on their submarines.

The big battle off Jutland gave the Germans an unexpected bonus. On May 28, prior to the clash of the fleets, a German U-boat had laid a mine field near the Orkney Islands to hamper British naval movements in that area. The mines did not affect the fighting; but on June 5, five days after the engagement, one of them struck England a bad blow.

The British war minister, Lord Horatio Herbert Kitchener, was traveling to Russia aboard the fast cruiser H.M.S. *Hampshire*. Foul weather caused the ship to veer off toward the Orkneys where she blundered into the mine field and struck a deadly missile. The *Hampshire* went down with nearly all hands, and Kitchener died in the raging waters.

The old hero's death came at a time when his prestige was at an ebb. There had been too many blunders made and too many men killed for Englishmen to look upon Kitchener with the admiration they had once shown.

Kitchener was a nineteenth-century soldier. Fierce, dashing, bold, he simply did not understand the nature of the world war. But he had a talent for organization and left behind a fine monument, the new mass British Army of volunteers and conscripts which he had created and trained.

Shortly after his death, these magnificent troops were thrown into an attack which became one of the blackest pages in English military history. Papa Joffre and General Sir Douglas Haig chose to hit the Germans in the Somme sector where the British and French armies linked up.

They could not have made a worse selection. For nearly two years the Germans had been strengthening their lines at the Somme. Dugouts were deep, trenches well built, barbed wire aprons thick and tangled. Every foot of ground was covered by machine-gun fire. Concrete pillboxes and bunkers guarded the approaches to the German lines.

The complex defensive system ran to a depth of several kilometers; farmhouses and barns had been converted into strongpoints; pleasant arbors concealed artillery batteries. The picturesque villages had been fortified. An intelligence report described the Somme sector as "the strongest and most perfectly defended region in the world."

Yet, the Allied military planners, miles from the front in their comfortable headquarters, ignored the obvious fact that the Germans were so well entrenched in the Somme sector that any attack there was predoomed. Haig and Joffre stubbornly insisted on carrying it out and overruled every objection.

Fourteen British divisions supported by five French divisions were massed along a front approximately twenty miles long. Cannon of varying caliber began pounding the German lines on June 22, while overhead swarms of French and British pursuit planes drove off German aircraft. The Nieuports and Sopwiths swooped low to strafe enemy rear areas and communications trenches.

The infantry attack was scheduled to jump off on June 29 but was postponed by rain until July 1. General Haig's headquarters buzzed with confident talk as "zero hour" approached. The shelling was making a shambles of the German lines. Aerial scouts reported, "Whole portions of the enemy front are obscured by shell explosions."

On Saturday, July 1, at 7:30 A.M., the barrage rose to fresh intensity. The range was lengthened and the German second line came under the battering of the projectiles. Whistles shrilled in the British trenches and shock troops went "over the top" (each man carrying almost sixty pounds of equipment). The moment had come to "reap the victory," according to Haig.

The general anticipated no trouble. He was certain the artillery had "smashed the Hun in his lair." To exploit the expected breakthrough by the infantry, Haig had mobilized cavalry for swift action. The horsemen would raid the German rear once the line had been breached.

No such opportunity arose. Despite the merciless shelling, the barbed wire had not been cut, nor was the enemy annihilated. The Germans had survived the bombardment in bunkers, trenches and dugouts. Observers in deep shelters watched the British lines through periscopes.

When the barrage lifted and the Tommies started forward, German machine gunners had a field day spraying the oncoming ranks with lead. The British advanced in waves, shoulder to shoulder, crossing no man's land at a slow walk. Men fell in squads and platoons; but still the stubborn Tommies pressed on. They even took a few German trenches, only to be driven out by counterattacks.

Before the sun went down that hot summer day 60,000 Englishmen had been killed, wounded or captured. It was the worst day for the British Army in any war before or since.

That same Saturday, the French also attacked. In that sector, the Germans were taken by surprise. They had not believed the French capable of offensive action with the fighting going on at Verdun. But Joffre's men made only limited advances, and the Battle of the Somme dragged on into the fall and winter without any appreciable gains being made.

On September 15, the British uncovered a weapon which sent a shudder through the German Army. From lowliest private to field marshal, the mighty *Reichswehr* quaked in its jackboots.

That day a British attack by twelve divisons battered the German positions. In most sectors the advancing troops used orthodox tactics—a barrage followed by infantry. Some sorties were repulsed, others made small gains. But at one point, startled Germans saw lumbering at them out of the morning mists huge, clanking metallic vehicles with machine guns spitting fire and six-pounders blasting. Barbed wire was flattened by the caterpillar treads which propelled the armored monsters over shell holes and across trenches.

Close behind the strange machines came files of Tommies with bayoneted rifles. The Germans frantically emptied belts of ammunition at the oncoming behemoths. The bullets merely rattled off the steel sides, and before the frightened

Germans knew it, the Tommies were down upon them with grenades and bayonets.

Word flashed back from the front lines to German Army headquarters. "The English have an infernal machine we can not stop!" The Kaiser's soldiers had been introduced to the tank: the most startling innovation in land warfare yet devised.

The armored juggernaut had been predicted in a story by H. G. Wells back in 1903. Even before that Leonardo da Vinci had foreseen a similar type of war vehicle. But in 1915, Lieutenant Colonel Ernest Dunlap Swinton of the Royal Engineers had drawn up a practicable plan for an armored gun-carrier.

Swinton showed his idea to Winston Churchill, then First Lord of the Admiralty, who became so enthused that he obtained permission to build the new weapon. Originally called a "land cruiser," it was later given the name "tank" to preserve secrecy.

Their first time in action, tanks proved themselves worthy. Forty-nine had reached France by September 15, but only thirty-six actually went into combat; the rest were disabled by mechanical difficulties. Of those that took part in the fighting, one captured a fortified village, and the crew of another took three hundred prisoners. Not a single tank was put out of commission by the Germans.

Just as the Germans had blundered with poison gas, the British had unveiled the tanks too soon. The men who handled them were not fully trained; nor were tactics properly developed. The vehicles were mechanically imperfect.

"If only we had waited until better tanks were ready and tank techniques perfected, those armored monsters might have broken the bloody stalemate and won the war for us," a British staff officer regretted. The generals had fumbled again. Instead of victory, the tanks merely brought a glimmer of hope to the men in the muddy trenches.

The Battle of the Somme went on until the torrential rains of October and November made the battlefield a quagmire and no further operations could be carried out in that sector. Joffre's and Haig's grand offensive ended in mud, misery and cold. The British lost 410,000 of that country's finest young men; France gave 200,000 sons at the Somme plus those who fell at Verdun. The Germans paid with 800,000 killed and wounded. That year, the winter winds sweeping across northern France were tainted by the stench of death.

7

"WE HAVE SAVED RUSSIA!"

THE BATTLES OF VERDUN AND THE SOMME SHOOK THE WEST-
ern front, and their reverberations were felt in Russia. That
nation, which seemed to have been mortally wounded at
the end of 1915, found new strength by March, 1916.

A new railway line from Murmansk to Petrograd carried
needed supplies and arms shipped from England. More
equipment and weapons arrived by way of Vladivostok along
the Trans-Siberian Railroad.

Russia never had any shortages of brave men; only material
was lacking. Now the Army's ranks again swelled with recruits. French and British officers came to train the fresh
troops, and for the first time since the war's onset the Russian Army was in prime fighting trim.

Unhappily, the Verdun situation brought a desperate
call to Tsar Nicholas for a Russian offensive which might
relieve enemy pressure in the West. Nicholas ordered his
generals to attack at once. An improvised drive was hurled
against strongly entrenched Germans in the Pripet Marshes.

"Before the spring flowers bloom, you will have crushed
the foe," a Russian colonel promised his regiment.

The attack lasted from March 16 to March 28. During
those twelve days, 100,000 Russians fell under German artillery and machine guns. The marshes became "a vast Russian cemetery," according to a German observer.

But the spring fiasco was followed by a great summer

success. On June 4, General Alexi Brusilov, a brilliant cavalry officer who had risen to command an army group, hurled a thunderbolt against the Austrians along a 200-mile-wide sector of the Galician front.

This attack was made in response to an Italian appeal to draw strength from an Austrian offensive that was breaking through in northern Italy. Since the best and most reliable Austrian troops had been transferred from Galicia to Italy, Brusilov's attack split the Austrian lines wide open.

Fiery Brusilov passed on some of his own spark to the troops. The common Russian soldier was splendid in this action. For once, he was not merely cannon fodder, but had weapons, supplies and leadership. Brusilov's men relished the taste of victory.

By the end of June, Brusilov had shattered two Austrian armies and recaptured many square miles of territory. Franz Josef's demoralized troops surrendered by regiments. Czechs and other minorities in the Austro-Hungarian Army deserted to the Russians and volunteered to fight their Austrian masters.

Church bells clanged throughout Russia hailing the news of the triumphs. Brusilov became a national hero whose picture hung in shop windows and homes all over Russia. His victories forced the Austrians to cancel their Italian drive and rush divisions to Galicia. Thousands of German reinforcements poured in from the West to plug the gaps in the Austrian lines. But not even these additional forces stopped Brusilov. The Russians advanced all through the summer, and the ripening Galician wheat fields were crimson with the blood of thousands killed on both sides.

As resistance stiffened, Russian casualties rose higher, but Brusilov kept driving ahead. Had he been properly supported, his men might have poured through the Carpathian passes into both Hungary and Austria. Franz Josef's empire tottered on the verge of catastrophe. Only a few more blows would have brought it down in ruins.

The knockout punch was never delivered. The petty jealousies, incompetence and stupidity that robbed Brusilov of his deserved victory temporarily saved Austro-Hungary and planted the seeds of revolution in the hearts and minds of the Russian soldier.

The average Russian now felt he had been betrayed by his leaders. Brusilov's soldiers went without needed equipment because others, envious of his successes, held back the flow of matériel earmarked for him.

The Russian troops again had to attack barehanded. They had cannon without shells, rifles with ammunition of the wrong caliber. Food rotted in railroad sidings for lack of transport, and while men at the front went hungry, behind the lines rear-echelon officers ate caviar and drank French champagne.

Brusilov's offensive petered out early in September when the leaves were turning scarlet and golden and the earth was white with early frost. This was Russia's greatest effort of the war; it had regained much territory and inflicted serious casualties on the enemy.

At the height of the Russian forward thrust, when it seemed Austria would soon fall, Rumania entered the war on the Allied side. Had the Rumanians moved quickly, they could have invaded Austria over a virtually undefended frontier; but they hesitated until the end of August. Brusilov had been stopped by then, and the Rumanian Army, 500,000 strong, was crushed by a combination of Austrian, German, Turkish and Bulgarian troops. In less than four months, more than three-quarters of the country was overrun. Remnants of the Rumanian Army fell back to the Sereth River and linked up with Russian forces. By December the Rumanian capital, Bucharest, was taken, and the campaign was virtually finished.

Ironically, the Brusilov offensive, which had promised to bring victory, irrevocably doomed the Tsar and led to the Bolshevik (Communist) revolution of 1917. One million Russian casualties resulted from the grand attack. The Dark People, who mourned their dead, now looked upon Nicholas with hatred. They cursed the Little Father they once had revered.

The Russian Empire was in its death throes, but so was the Austro-Hungarian Empire. On November 22, Franz Josef died at the age of eighty-six; he had ruled for sixty-eight years. His successor, Karl, brother of Archduke Ferdinand, was destined to rule only two years.

Hoping to salvage something, Emperor Karl tried to persuade the Germans to mediate a peace agreement through the Pope. But Kaiser Wilhelm had gone too far along the road to permit such a peace; nor would his generals hear of it. They felt Germany was on the threshold of outright victory.

"We must not let weaklings throw away what we have won with our blood!" a staff officer declared.

The generals ignored the misery and want blighting every German home. They were blinded by ambition for Germany and clung to the delusion that victory was within reach. The generals saw themselves as the architects of a new and great Germany. Today, Europe! Tomorrow, the world! *Deutschland, Deutschland über alles!* This was their dream, and to attain it, Germans had to sacrifice more sons, more wealth, more strength.

The dream was a mad one. The men who sought to carry it out were demented by the lust for power. The German nation no longer behaved rationally. Because the Kaiser believed the dream, so did his subjects. Only cowards and traitors doubted.

If the Germans deluded themselves, so did a group of young Russian noblemen who thought they could stave off disaster by murdering the insidious monk Rasputin. They believed his baleful influences were destroying the country.

These young patriotic aristocrats refused to see that their way of life was ended. They clung to the hope that the Little Father could lead Russia to victory if Rasputin's spell over him was broken. Convinced of this, they lured the monk out of the royal palace in Petrograd on a bitterly cold December night and murdered him.

Rasputin died hard; he survived stabbing, poisoning and shooting. While he still breathed, his killers dragged him to a stream, chopped a hole in the ice and threw him into the frigid water. The ice soon closed over Rasputin and sealed him beneath the surface.

The news of what had occurred spread through Petrograd. The telegraph carried word to Moscow. Jubliant people poured into the streets. Rasputin was dead! Long live the Tsar! Now the Little Father was free! Now Russia could march!

"We have saved Russia!" one of Rasputin's murderers exulted. But the death of a shrewd intriguer who preyed on superstitious minds could not save Russia from her black destiny. Rasputin was only a symptom of what ailed that unhappy land. The disease was incurable. The Dark People were stirring. Everything in their path was fated to be swept away by the swirling currents of their hatred.

8

"HE KEPT US OUT OF WAR!"

AMONG THE MANY NOTABLE FIGURES, BOTH POLITICAL AND military, who disappeared from the spotlight in 1916 was Papa Joffre. Premier Aristide Briand of France kicked him upstairs with the rank of field marshal and sent the old soldier into forced retirement. The failure at the Somme and the bloodletting of Verdun ended Joffre's active army career.

His successor, General Robert Nivelle, was an arrogant, boastful man. Nivelle bragged he would "bring the *boche* to heel" and promised to "sweep out the invader before the winter of 1917." His bombast was to bring France still more grief and drive the *poilus* beyond endurance.

Herbert Asquith, England's Prime Minister, also fell from power. The British people demanded a change in the government. They had given much in the two years of war, and 1916 marked their breaking point.

Even the solid English could no longer put up with the traditional "muddling through" of the past two years. Food costs had risen intolerably. Coal was scarce, clothing expensive, and life for the average Briton had become extremely difficult.

German submarines preyed off the British Isles, and no day passed without ship sinkings. Zeppelins pounded coastal towns, and Londoners were becoming accustomed to air raids. Trouble seethed in southern Ireland, and during Easter week, 1916, a full-scale rebellion broke out. It was crushed after much bloodshed and ruthless military action.

The situation in England offered small comfort; black crepe hung on thousands of doors to mourn a son, husband, brother or sweetheart. The way ahead seemed endless and hopeless. It became obvious that Herbert Asquith was not the man who could lead the nation to victory. Amid mounting protests, a new Prime Minister rose to power.

The man to whom the British people turned was David Lloyd George, a dynamic Welshman who spoke out for the common man. George hated the military bunglers who had made so many mistakes; he was determined to end what he called "battlefield idiocy."

Led by peppery Lloyd George, the average Englishman tightened his belt, gritted his teeth and "got on with it," confident that the Prime Minister would "make the Hun pay."

The United States was also beset with problems in the war-torn world. President Woodrow Wilson faced growing demands to prepare the tiny U.S. Army for national defense. General Leonard Wood, a distinguished soldier, led the rising sentiment. He pointed out that the United States had virtually no armed forces. Less than 200,000 men (including reserves) formed the Army. Of these only 92,000 were regulars; the rest, partially trained National Guardsmen.

"Should an emergency arise," General Wood warned, "we could not protect ourselves. The time is past when citizens can become soldiers overnight. Today, it takes more than a rifle to make a fighting man. We need trained troops and plenty of them!"

Many patriotic Americans, alarmed by the country's military impotence, listened to General Wood and decided something must be done. Preparedness organizations mushroomed across the United States in 1916. One university and college after another adopted military training programs.

A "businessmen's camp" was set up at Plattsburg, New York, where earnest men (many of them middle-aged) sweated through basic infantry drill. Among the "trainees" were socialities, corporation executives, journalists and actors.

In 1916, the United States had further reasons for enlarging its army. On March 9 of that year, a band of about 1,500 Mexican soldiers led by General Pancho Villa raided across the border into Columbus, New Mexico. They shot up the town and attacked the nearby camp of the 13th U.S. Cavalry, inflicting numerous casualties.

The Columbus affair brought a strong reaction from President Wilson. He sent into Mexico a 6,000-man brigade commanded by Brigadier General John F. Pershing, who had orders to capture Villa and return him to the United States for trial.

Fifty-six-year old Pershing, called "Black Jack" by the troops, had seen fighting against hostile Indians on the western frontier and in the Spanish-American War. Although Black Jack pushed his mission energetically, it was slated for failure from the outset.

Villa's irregulars scattered into the rugged mountains of northern Mexico, and Pershing's troops found no trace of them. If the Americans had been equipped with aircraft to search mountain slopes and inaccessible passes, they might have had a chance. But Pershing had no planes, and his men pushed ever deeper into Mexico without achieving the least success.

The presence of American troops on Mexican soil aroused widespread anti-"Gringo" sentiment. The Mexicans grew increasingly hostile, and several times threatened to declare war. Pershing handled the tense situation with such skill and tact that no serious consequences resulted, although a clash with Mexican forces did take place in late June, 1916. Twenty-three U.S. cavalry troopers were captured, and tension ran high as Wilson mobilized more troops at the Rio Grande. However, the Mexicans released their captives, and Pershing plodded on through heat and dust on the trail of the elusive Villa.

In January, 1917, the U.S. War Department finally decided to call a halt. Pershing was ordered home and the last American soldier left Mexican territory by early February.

"We had nothing to show for nearly a year's work except sore feet and sunburns," one of Pershing's men remarked.

He underestimated the military benefits of the Mexican Border Campaign. A force of infantry and cavalry had undergone rigorous training in the field under combat conditions. Staff and line officers, noncoms and privates, gained invaluable experience.

The fact that Pershing failed to catch even a glimpse of Villa lowered American prestige, particularly in Germany, where certain groups regarded the United States as a potential enemy.

"There is nothing to fear from the Americans," a German military attaché in Washington wrote to Berlin. "Their army is ludicrous, not fit even to round up a gang of bandits."

Since the start of the war, the Germans had displayed an attitude of contempt toward America's armed forces. As the conflict spread and intensified, the Kaiser's government became increasingly scornful of the American Army and Navy. However, the United States industrial capacity caused concern in Germany. American munitions factories and machine shops were turning out quantities of war matériel for the Allies.

Since Britain controlled the seaways, a "bridge of ships" spanned the Atlantic, carrying the "tools of war" to England and France. The U-boats had not been able to stop the ships, and the Germans took drastic steps to choke off the flow of supplies from the United States to the Allies.

Mysterious fires damaged American factories and warehouses loaded with supplies for the Allies. Explosions of suspicious origins spread havoc. The worst such occurrence was on July 30 at Black Tom Island, off Jersey City, New Jersey, where a dynamite blast that took two lives and wreaked $40 million damage was set off by German agents.

Saboteurs planted time bombs on outward-bound merchantmen sailing for England. No one knew how many munitions-laden vessels, presumed lost to U-boats, had actually been blown up by hidden bombs. The Germans used every means to impede, slow down or cripple American factories filling war contracts for the Allies.

Some people in the United States believed that the Germans were justified. "America is not neutral," wrote an American-born German propagandist in New York City. "Let Uncle Sam stop doing business with the British and the so-called sabotage will cease at once!"

To arguments that Germany was at liberty to place war orders in America, a pro-German editor declared: "What a joke! That is the same as telling a man without legs to walk. The British have the ships. Germany has none. How is it possible to carry munitions from America to Germany?"

American business grew fat on Allied war orders. More men than ever before were at work. Munitions plants and factories, built with British and French money, went up along the Atlantic seaboard.

Europe's catastrophe was bringing prosperity to the United States, and only the most squeamish felt guilty about becoming "war millionaires." Of course, not every American was growing rich, and the majority regarded the war as an abomination. Most Americans were thankful that after two years the United States still stood on the side lines of the conflict.

However, many Americans were in the fighting. Scores of adventure-loving young men went off to Canada where they enlisted in the Royal Canadian Air Force. Other youths served in the British Army or the French Foreign Legion. The most famous of the American volunteers were a score of daredevil airmen flying for the French. Known as "The Lafayette Escadrille," they performed heroic feats over the western front in their speedy fighter planes.

There were no Americans known to be serving in the Kaiser's forces. Somehow, the German cause did not hold any appeal for idealists and romantic soldiers-of-fortune. Americans had long been soured by the heavy-handed brutality of German troops in Belgium, the cruel U-boat campaigns and the irritating arrogance of the Germans.

In 1916, Americans had to make a difficult domestic decision; one that would decide the nation's future for many years to come. A presidential election was at hand, and the voters were faced with adhering to Woodrow Wilson's policies or throwing him over.

The Republicans nominated a pair of distinguished candidates—Charles Evans Hughes, an Associate Justice of the Supreme Court, for President, and Charles Warren Fairbanks as his running mate. Hughes had prestige, intelligence and integrity. He was a good match for Wilson.

Wilson's supporters raised the slogan, "He kept us out of war!" Democratic spokesmen told the voters: "You are working, not fighting! You are alive and happy; not cannon fodder! If you want war, vote for Hughes. If you want peace with honor and continued prosperity, vote for Wilson."

Wilson was brilliant in the pre-election campaigning. He made a key speech which swung many voters to his side: "If the Republican party is put in power at the coming election, our foreign policy will be radically changed. They say all our policy is wrong. . . . If it is wrong . . . they must change it. . . . There is only one choice as against peace and that is war."

Wilson was elected by one of the slimmest margins in American history. He polled 9,129,606 popular votes against 8,538,221 for Hughes. The count in the electoral college was 277–254. The Wilson administration had been given another four-year mandate, and the college professor turned President now faced the task of living up to the slogan, "He kept us out of war!"

He was the helmsman of a ship sailing through black and stormy waters. Rocks and shoals threatened on either side, and the safe channel was daily growing narrower.

PART THREE

« 1917–1918 »
THE LAST FULL MEASURE

Till the war drum throbbed no longer
and the battle flags were furled
In the Parliament of Man, the Federation
of the world.
ALFRED, LORD TENNYSON, *Locksley Hall*

1

"JOHNNY GET YOUR GUN!"

ON AUGUST 6, 1914, IN THE WEEK THE WAR STARTED, PERSONAL
tragedy struck Woodrow Wilson, the twenty-eighth President
of the United States. His wife, Ellen, to whom he had been
married for twenty-nine years, died in the White House
after a long illness.

Wilson, a reserved man, revealed no outward signs of his
feelings. Instead he masked his grief and carried on with the
duties of office. Political enemies seized on this trait to paint
him as an "icy intellectual bereft of human emotions." But
those closest to Wilson knew differently. "He is torn by
sorrow . . . only his iron will permits him to function," an
aide said.

Because Wilson was a scholar he understood the scope
and nature of the war far better than did most men. The
United States needed leadership in the critical times ahead.
Although a President may be saddened and depressed, events
could not wait for his mood to change. So he buried his wife
and turned to the difficult problems of keeping the United
States neutral in a warring world. The President worked
selflessly and tirelessly to that end. It was a grueling task
and from the day of Mrs. Wilson's death until his second
term ended in March, 1921, Wilson did not pass an un-
troubled hour.

He remarried in December, 1915. His second wife, Elizabeth Bolling Galt, the widow of a wealthy Washington jeweler, was many years younger than he. The marriage gave his enemies another chance to attack him. Wilson was characterized as a heartless man for taking another wife so soon after the death of his first mate.

His foes and the yellow press tried to stir up a scandal, but their efforts fell flat. Most Americans felt that the President's private life was his own business. Besides, the climate in the United States was not right for gossip. Events were moving so rapidly that even the dullest person could foresee a showdown with Germany in the offing.

Incident after incident of German-inspired sabotage cropped up, and a deep-rooted antipathy toward Germany arose in the country. Newspaper and magazine writers stressed that Germany victory in the war would put both the British and French navies in the Kaiser's hands. A journalist wrote in a widely read magazine article:

> Wilhelm II is power mad and ambitious. . . . He envisions himself as another Alexander, a second Napoleon. . . . Is it beyond the realm of reason to suppose his lust for power will reach across the Atlantic? With history's greatest navy at his beck, what is there to stop this modern Attila from swooping down upon our shores? Logically, we are the new world for him to conquer should Britain and France fall. . . .

The same writer also reviewed the old fears of the "Yellow Peril." This he saw in the emergence of Japan, that country which had displayed a voracious appetite for territorial gain by grabbing German-owned islands in the Pacific. The article continued:

> . . . we must be alive to the possibility that a triumphant

Kaiser may one day persuade the Mikado to join him in attacking the United States. . . . Our nation's future is endangered by such a prospect.

Americans began having serious thoughts about the shape of things to come if these predictions proved true. Another important fact influenced the American attitude toward Germany. By 1917, United States bankers had loaned the Allies more than two billion dollars. Should Britain and France fall, this vast sum would never be repaid, and no man could foretell how such a loss might damage future American economy.

Thus, in many ways, the American people were drifting into a pattern of conflict with Germany. Allied propaganda skillfully kept alive tales of German atrocities: wild yarns about Canadian prisoners being "crucified," of women and children mutilated by German troops and fiendish crimes committed against innocent civilians in Belgium and France.

During 1915, the Germans put to death a British-born nurse, Miss Edith Cavell, for helping Allied captives escape from prisoner-of-war camps in Belgium. That same year the French executed nine women as German spies, including the exotic dancer Mata Hari. Very few Americans knew the French had stood women before firing squads. But everyone in the United States was aware of Edith Cavell's unhappy fate. The mere mention of her name evoked growls about "murdering Huns" and "dirty *boches.*"

But if Allied propagandists did much to win American sympathy, German behavior did even more. The military and naval attachés of the German embassy at Washington, D.C., Captains Franz von Papen and Karl von Boy-Ed, and the Austrian ambassador, Dr. Constantine Dumba, were ordered by the U.S. State Department to leave the country for financing and guiding the work of sabotage, espionage and arson rings.

This German behavior was bad enough, but it was topped in February, 1917. Late that month, Alfred Zimmermann, a German under-secretary of foreign affairs, sent a coded message to the Kaiser's ambassador in Mexico. The British secret service intercepted and decoded the dispatch. The contents were so startling that the British lost no time getting them to Walter Hines Page, the American ambassador at London, who immediately rushed the note to Secretary of State Robert Lansing.

The so-called Zimmermann Note created an uproar when it was made public. On behalf of his government, Zimmermann promised that should Mexico go to war with the United States, Germany would help her recover Texas, New Mexico and Arizona, the territory lost to the United States in the Mexican War of 1845–1848.

The Zimmmermann Note came at a time when relations between Germany and the United States were already strained to the limit. On January 31,1917, Count von Bernstorff, the German ambassador in Washington, handed Secretary of State Lansing a letter stating Germany's intent to renew unrestricted submarine warfare the following day.

The U-boats were to sink ships of any nation found in British waters. Only one exception would be made: the United States could send a passenger vessel every week to England, provided she went to Falmouth and nowhere else, arrived there on a Sunday, left on a Wednesday, traveled a specified course and was marked with alternate red and white stripes on her hull and superstructure. The ship also had to fly at each masthead a large flag checkered white and red, in addition to the American flag at her stern. The United States government also was obliged to pledge that the ship carried no contraband, according to a list compiled by the Germans.

This edict was too much for Americans to swallow. Protests rose across the country. "These orders could not be more tyrannical if German armies held every foot of our nation from the Atlantic to Pacific!" a Chicago newspaper stated in an angry editorial. "This is the good old U.S.A., not occupied Belgium! No despot can order us about!"

"What sort of men do the Germans think we are? Do they really believe we shall decorate our ships like barber poles or fly flags resembling kitchen tablecloths, because they tell us we must!" John Bach McMaster, an eminent historian, asked a reporter.

There were many harsh comments made about the conditions imposed by the Germans, but none summed up the feelings of the average American better than a remark uttered by a longshoreman on a New York pier: "So the Kaiser says we can send only one ship a week to England, huh? I say he can go to Hell every day!"

The German proclamation of unrestricted submarine warfare shocked Wilson. He had been recently rebuffed by the belligerents in December, 1916, after suggesting that the warring nations should accept "peace without victory" and offering to negotiate the settlement. His hope of becoming the world's peacemaker was shattered when England, France, Germany and their allies turned him down.

Now, early in 1917, Wilson was forced to act. The German terms were intolerable. The new reign of U-boat *schrecklichkeit* (terror) was unbearable. Wilson determined to show the Kaiser that the President of the United States was no "meek schoolmaster."

On February 3, 1917, he stood before Congress and declared: "I have directed the Secretary of State to announce to his Excellency the German Ambassador, that all diplomatic relations between the United States and the German Empire are severed. . . ."

The speech was completed at 2:00 P.M. About five minutes later, Count von Bernstorff was handed his passport. German consuls at various points around the United States were summoned to Washington. On February 14, von Bernstorff and 149 others sailed from New York aboard a Danish vessel. The United States and Germany had moved closer to conflict.

In mid-March, after German U-boats torpedoed three American freighters, President Wilson called a special joint session of Congress to convene on Monday, April 2, 1917, "to receive a communication concerning grave matters."

That day, a grave President stood before a packed House of Representatives and said: "The present German submarine warfare is a warfare against mankind. . . . There is one choice we cannot make, we are incapable of making: we will not choose the path of submission. . . ."

The audience rose as one and cheered him. An observer noted, "Many in that crowd of senators, congressmen, Justices of the Supreme Court and cabinet members had tears streaming down their cheeks." The President went on: "We seek no indemnities . . . no material compensation . . . we desire no conquest, no dominion. . . . We have no selfish ends to serve. . . . The world must be made safe for democracy," President Wilson added. He concluded his speech by calling for war on Germany. "America is taking the only action possible. . . . God helping her, she can take no other!"

In this fashion and with these words, the United States went to war against Imperial Germany. On April 6, Congress voted that a state of war actually existed. Suddenly, sprawling, peaceful America was at war for the first time since 1898. All at once, the distant guns sounded omniously loud.

The reaction of the American people was a violent one. Everything German was condemned, often illogically: sauerkraut became "liberty cabbage"; frankfurters, "hot dogs"; and dachshunds, "liberty hounds"; stores, shops and homes owned by Germans were stoned and even burned.

Only a year before, people had been singing, "I Didn't Raise My Boy to Be a Soldier." In April, 1917, the most popular song was, "Johnny Get Your Gun!"

2

EXIT THE TSAR

ABOUT A MONTH BEFORE THE UNITED STATES ENTERED THE war, the social upheaval that had been brewing in Russia finally erupted with the fury of a volcano. At the start of the year, the Russian Army seemed stronger than ever. Despite the ghastly casualties, some six million men were in uniform (more than Russia had in 1914). British convoys hauled quantities of matériel to Murmansk where artillery, ammunition, rifles and machine guns were piled on the docks.

Some Allied observers felt Russia capable of carrying on still another year's campaign. She had troops, equipment and good commanders such as Brusilov. But her military power was broken. Her army was a shell that merely resembled a disciplined fighting force; beneath its martial surface, sedition and mutiny smoldered.

Morale was shattered. The soldiers no longer cared for Tsar or country. The errors, blunders and disasters of the past two years had destroyed their confidence. Men were no longer willing to die for the Little Father. "If we must give our lives, let it be for ourselves, our wives, our children and not for Nicholas, who has betrayed our faith in him," a soldier wrote from the front.

The winter of 1916–1917 had been particularly harsh, and the civilian populace suffered severely. Food and coal were scarce. In the courtyard of the Petrograd Winter Palace, where Nicholas and his followers lived opulently, one saw children scrabbling amidst scraps left over from a royal banquet. Infants died whimpering for milk. Old people were found frozen to death on doorsteps. Hunger stalked Russia, and the people called to the Tsar for help. But Nicholas paid no more attention to them than he did to the Arctic winds howling through Petrograd.

Blind and deaf to the mounting crisis, he ignored the suffering masses. The Tsar knew nothing of hunger and cold, of misery and want. His children were warm and well-fed. He dined on capon and caviar.

In the Duma (Parliament), Menshevik (Socialist) deputies spoke of overthrowing the Tsar and setting up a republic. In back alleys, basements and cellars, Bolshevik (Communist) agitators printed leaflets calling upon the people to revolt. Exiled Bolsheviks and Mensheviks sneaked back into Russia from the wastelands of Siberia. Josef Visorionovich Djugishivili, known as Josef Stalin (Man of Steel), a veteran revolutionary, came furtively from Siberia to stir the people to revolt.

Vladimir Ilyitch Ulanov, a Bolshevik leader who called himself Nicholas Lenin, awaited word in Switzerland that the Russian people had risen. Lenin had been banished from his homeland eleven years before but still held control of the Bolsheviks.

From his Swiss hideout, Lenin wrote, "The day is at hand . . . a revolutionary situation is arising . . . even at this distance, one can heart the anguished groans of suffering workers and peasants. . . . The day is at hand, comrades, and we must be ready to take over."

At a greater distance, in a Bronx, New York, flat, another Bolshevik leader, a writer, editor, actor and orator, Lev

Davidovich Bronstein, watched the flow of history in Russia. Bronstein, who was to win fame as Leon Trotsky, had fled to America to escape the Tsarist police. In New York City, he eked out a living by writing articles for the left-wing press and working as an extra in a Bronx movie studio. His disheveled hair, pointed beard and pince-nez glasses became familiar to neighbors on the street where he lived.

All over, men eagerly studied the signs of the coming storm over Russia. As they had throughout the years, the secret police ferreted out Bolshevik agitators in Petrograd, Moscow and other cities. Some they tortured, some they killed, others they sent off to Siberia.

But no police terror could break the revolutionary spirit throbbing in Russia. It reached to the remote villages, the factories, the farms. Sailors in the fleet were infected by the anti-Tsarist venom; soldiers at the front refused to obey orders. Firing squads and prisons could not stem the tide of violent change.

The Tsar stubbornly rejected all suggestions to democratize his regime. "We are the ruler of Holy Russia. We are the Father of Our people. God has chosen Us and no man may question Our ways," he said.

But men did question, and the questions grew more persistent. Conditions worsened. Crippling strikes broke out in factories and machine shops. The speeches in the Duma became more subversive; the deputies now constantly spoke of forcing the Tsar from the throne.

On March 11, Tsar Nicholas, at Army headquarters in Pskov, ordered the Duma to disband. The deputies disobeyed him and defiantly called a meeting. Troops, including several Cossack regiments, were rushed to Petrograd; the fierce Tartar horsemen had always been loyal to the Tsar.

Great crowds formed in the streets. Mobs surged toward

the Winter Palace, shouting for bread. A Cossack troop charged with whips, sabers and bullets. The demonstrators scattered. Those who had weapons fought back. Homemade bombs exploded among the Cossacks. Rioting broke out all over the capital. Street barricades fashioned from paving blocks, overturned trucks and wagons, cars and carriages, blocked off whole sections of the city. Red flags blossomed throughout Petrograd.

The revolution had begun and thousands upon thousands of Russians welcomed it. They sang "The Marseillaise" and "The Internationale." Everywhere one heard revolutionary songs.

Soldiers refused to fire on the people; one guards regiment shot its officers and went over to the mob. Most troops merely stood aside and watched. Menshevik deputies hurried from the Duma to organize and lead the masses.

All through the night of March 11–12 (February 26–27 by the Russian-style Gregorian calendar) fires burned in Petrograd. Red was the outstanding color. The sky was tinted red by flames; the trampled snow stained crimson; and blood-red flags flapped in the sharp wind.

Some regiments still backed Nicholas. The household bodyguard and the Officers' Corps of Cadets fought mutinous troops and populace and were annihilated. Artillery thudded in the streets, glass shattered, rifle shots cracked and machine guns chattered.

The revolution spread from Petrograd to Moscow and the countryside. Political prisoners were released from jail. Soon, every street corner in Petrograd had its throng harangued by speakers advising the people to do this or that. No one group was quite ready to take power when the Tsar suddenly abdicated at 3:00 P.M., March 15.

Standing in his Pskov headquarters, Nicholas glumly faced

a committee of Menshevik deputies who had come to demand his resignation. "God help Russia," he said, as he gave up the throne.

The following day, the Tsar's uncle, Grand Duke Nicholas, was offered the crown, but refused to accept it. Menshevik members of the Duma Executive Committee, including several liberal noblemen, formed a provisional government headed by Prince G. E. Lvov. In the cabinet was a Menshevik lawyer named Alexander Kerensky, who served as Minister of Justice.

To safeguard the new government and discourage a pro-Tsarist counterrevolution, Prince Lvov ordered Nicholas and his family arrested. They were held in "protective custody" at Tsarkoe Selo, the royal summer home. (In April, 1918 the royal family was removed to Ekaterinburg in the Urals where, on July 16, the Tsar, his wife and children were executed by the Bolsheviks, and the Romanoff dynasty ended forever.)

The provisional government had rough sailing from the start. Its authority was immediately challenged by Bolshevik-inspired Workers and Soldiers Councils, or Soviets. These militant groups called for an end to the war and denounced Lvov's government as "capitalist warmongers" because the Prince felt obligated to continue fighting Germany.

The Petrograd Soviet raised the slogan, "Peace, Bread and Land!" the immediate needs of the Russian people. The offer of land won over to the Bolshevik side the Russian peasant, whose age-old ambition had been to farm a parcel of his own.

Soviets were formed in the Army and the Navy. Mutiny and desertion spread like a smallpox epidemic. Everywhere along the front, the Russian armies began to dissolve. But some divisions still held firm, and the Germans, hoping to get Russia out of the war for good, enlisted an unlikely ally in an attempt to win complete victory without any further effort on their part.

The German high command arranged to transport Nicholas Lenin in a sealed train from Switzerland, across Germany into Russia. A wild demonstration greeted Lenin in the Petrograd railroad station. The Soviets now had the leader they needed. Lenin was soon joined by other devoted Bolsheviks: Lev B. Kamenev, Grigori Zinoviev, Vyacheslev Molotov, Leon Trotsky and Josef Stalin; with these men Lenin plotted the overthrow of the provisional government. (Ironically, each of Lenin's closest aides eventually fell into disfavor. Kamenev and Zinoviev died before Communist firing squads; Trotsky was murdered; and Stalin was downgraded by the Khrushchev regime. Only Lenin's memory remains untarnished).

After Lenin's return, the provisional government really ran into stormy weather. Kerensky rose to become War and Navy Minister, and in July was made Prime Minister. Gathering an army of Siberian and Finnish troops (the least affected by Bolshevik propaganda), he launched an offensive in Galicia under Generals Brusilov and Kornilov.

The attack was doomed from its inception. Soviets in the Army ordered the men to disobey their officers. Wholesale desertions weakened the lines, and the Germans advanced at will. Kerensky still tried to keep his armies fighting; but it was no use. Before long, his regime wavered and then toppled on November 7–8, as a Bolshevik uprising, led by Lenin and Trotsky, took place.

Mutinous sailors from the Kronstadt Naval Base, armed workers formed into militia units called the Red Guard, rebellious troops and thousands of ordinary citizens overthrew the Kerensky government. A feeble attempt was made to hold the Winter Palace, the seat of Kerensky's cabinet, but the only forces to defend it were some women soldiers and boys from the Officers' Cadet School.

Kerensky escaped while shots echoed through the war-torn streets of Petrograd. The Bolsheviks seized the reins of government, and the Duma was dissolved as Trotsky stood on the podium shouting at the deputies: "Your role is played out. Go where you belong—on the rubbish heap of history!"

Under Lenin, the Bolsheviks set up the so-called Dictatorship of the Proletariat—a working class government, sworn to destroy the capitalist system in accordance with the tenets of Karl Marx, the Father of Communism, who long before had warned, ". . . a specter is stalking Europe . . . the specter of Communism."

That specter was no longer an imaginary one. It was real enough. Russia was in the hands of the Communists. The transition from Tsarism to the Dictatorship of the Proletariat came violently. Civil war raged between the Reds (Bolsheviks) and the Whites (anti-Bolsheviks). (That civil war would last from 1917 until 1921, and before it finished, not only Russians, but also Czech, Finnish, Polish, British, American, French and Japanese troops were to participate in the fighting.)

In November, 1917, Lenin made overtures to the Germans for withdrawing Russia from the war. By December 22, 1917, an armistice was arranged at Brest-Litovsk, on stiff German terms, at which Leon Trotsky, the Soviet representative, balked. However, the Russians had no alternative but to accept the harsh German demands. "The only choice you have," a German official told Trotsky, "is as to what sort of sauce we shall eat you with."

To save Russia from a full-scale German invasion, Trotsky accepted the Treaty of Brest-Litovsk, which ceded Finland, the Baltic provinces, Poland, the Ukraine and other areas, either to Germany or German-backed governments.

With Russia out of the war, Rumania also had to surrender. She, too, lost much territory, and for the first time since 1914, the Germans could fight a one-front war—in the West. The withdrawal of Russia freed 100 German divisions for service in France and Belgium—but the Bolshevik Revolution was to have a more serious impact on the western front and the world than merely providing a source of seasoned reinforcements for the Germans.

3

"À BAS LA GUERRE!"

AT THE START OF 1917 BEFORE THE RUSSIAN REVOLUTION HAD
yet burst into full fury, the Allied high command planned
the year's strategy. The generals had grand ideas for 1917.
It was to be the decisive year. Simultaneous massive attacks
would be launched in the West, the East and Italy, with the
main blow falling on the western front. There, the Allies had
numerical superiority (4,000,000 against 2,500,000) including
three Russian brigades serving with the French, as concrete
evidence of Tsar Nicholas' solidarity with his allies.

Nobody then realized the irony of the Tsar sending troops
to help the British and French when in all the world there
was no help for him. The generals, unaware that Nicholas
and his regime were already doomed, pored over their maps
and talked of victory.

At the same time jackbooted, bemonocled German generals were also meeting and studying the maps. The Kaiser's
military chiefs decided to remain on the defensive in both the
East and the West while the U-boats waged an all-out effort to
paralyze England. The planners had shuffled the cards; it
now remained for history to deal them.

As the winter weather grudgingly gave way to spring,
General Robert Nivelle, the braggart who had replaced
Papa Joffre, made no secret of his intentions. Nivelle
boasted he would force a breakthrough on a wide front "by

direct assault," as though he had learned nothing from the awful slaughter of the past—the human waste of Flanders, the butchery of Verdun and the Somme. Because Nivelle had a convincing personality, men who should have known better became convinced he could smash the German lines with a head-on attack. However, at the peak of Nivelle's rash promises, the wily German, General Erich Ludendorff, under orders from General Paul von Hindenburg, forestalled the swashbuckling Frenchman by making a large-scale withdrawal in the very sector in which Nivelle had been planning his attack.

The Germans pulled back from the so-called Noyon bulge to a much shorter front that ran from Arras through St. Quentin to Laffoux, six miles east of Soissons. Ludendorff's "strategic withdrawal" reached a depth of thirty-one miles in some sectors and was the greatest movement made on the western front for three years.

Seldom was a military maneuver conducted with greater skill and control. The new German front could be held by fewer troops, which was the reason for the retirement—to conserve German manpower. The line to which Ludendorff fell back was a masterpiece of field fortifications. The deep trenches, which had connecting tunnels, were further strengthened by concrete pillboxes and dugouts. Interlacing machine-gun nests covered the denuded ground. The Germans called their ingenious defensive position the Siegfried Line to honor the mythical Teutonic hero, but soon renamed it the Hindenburg Line after their commanding general.

As the *Reichswehr* retreated, it carried out a scorched-earth policy and destroyed everything in its path. Towns, villages, even individual farmhouses were razed. No tree was left standing. Every road was torn up. The Germans poisoned wells and blocked streams. Booby traps were placed and fields mined. A newspaperman with Ludendorff said:

". . . he has created a man-made wasteland to match nature at her worst."

Nivelle shrugged when he heard what the enemy was doing. "The so-called Hindenburg Line is of no consequence. . . . I shall bury the Germans in their own trenches."

He discussed his coming offensive with an appalling lack of discretion. Details of it were common talk in every Paris café. "All a German spy need do is sit at a table in any *bistro* along the Champs Elysées and listen to the conversation. I daresay there is neither a chambermaid nor street sweeper in all France who does not know Nivelle means to attack the Germans between Soissons and Rheims by mid-April," a French intelligence officer complained.

As Nivelle went on bragging, the Germans oiled their machine guns and waited in the security of the Hindenburg Line. However, it was the British and not the French who started the annual slaughter on the western front.

In the slate-gray drizzle of Easter Monday, April 9, a few days after the United States had declared war, British troops went "over the top" along a twenty-mile-wide sector near Arras, where the Hindenburg Line's northwestern flank was anchored on razorbacked Vimy Ridge.

Determined not to fail this time, Sir Douglas Haig massed 2,817 pieces of artillery, 48 tanks and 450 airplanes to support his fourteen infantry divisions. The artillery kept up a week-long bombardment that began April 2 and lasted until April 9.

At the same time, British planes gained supremacy of the air. The pilots of the Royal Flying Corps dueled with the aces of Baron Manfred von Richtofen's famous "Flying Circus" and beat them. One of von Richtofen's squadron leaders was a chunky aviator named Hermann Goering, who would win infamy years later as a leader of Nazi Germany.

The British barrage shook the Germans at Arras, and the

Tommies rushed in so close behind the bursting shells that the enemy had no time to reorganize his defenses.

The Canadians fought gallantly to seize and hold Vimy Ridge. But Arras was only a limited victory, a two-to-five mile advance along the entire front. Once German artillery zeroed in and second-line defenses stiffend, the attack bogged down.

The battle lasted until April 24. During that time the British suffered more than 80,000 casualties while inflicting 57,000 on the Germans plus capturing 18,128 men and 230 guns.

Haig probably would have been satisfied to break off the battle after his initial gains, but he had to keep going to support General Nivelle's long-heralded blow, which fell while the fighting waxed at Arras. In the dismal dawn hours of Monday, April 16, General Nivelle sent a message to his troops: "The hour has come! Confidence. Courage! Long live France! The word is Forward!" This was the day the country had been awaiting; the day supposed to mark her march to victory.

Nivelle had fifty-four divisions to hurl against the Germans on a fifty-mile-wide front from Soissons to Rheims in the valley of the Aisne River. The assault opened with an artillery bombardment described as "awesome"—French guns rained eleven million shells on the enemy. The *poilus* went "over the top" with their traditional dash and *élan*; wave after wave of infantry in horizon blue uniforms, mingled with khaki-clad colonial troops, stumbled across the shell-torn ground. But the spirited attackers were cut down as they crossed No Man's Land. German machine-gun nests had been untouched by Nivelle's mammoth barrage. His much vaunted "end the war" breakthrough was stopped on the first day.

Nivelle refused to believe he had failed and threw more and still more men into the slaughtering ground. His *poilus* died by the hundreds to capture a 650-foot-high eminence called Chemin des Dames. Other gains were made at a sickening cost in lives. Conservative estimates were 167,000 casualties for the French Army from April 16 to 25.

Behind the lines, aid stations and hospitals were so crowded that the wounded had to lie unattended for hours, even days, on the muddy ground. "I have seen animals better treated," a war correspondent said. "The cries and groans of wounded men pierced me to my soul."

Still the battle went on, until suddenly, something incredible happened. On May 3, a division of Algerian troops refused to return to the front. *"À bas la guerre!"* (Down with the war!) the men chanted as they marched rearward.

The seeds of mutiny quickly took root, especially among troops on leave. Unit after unit refused to go to the front. The Communists were quick to act. They agitated among the soldiers, raising demands for a negotiated peace and a working class revolution in France.

Red flags flew in regiment after regiment, and the strains of "The Internationale" could be heard. Whole units demonstrated against the war, beat up military police, derailed troop trains, set fire to warehouses and supply dumps and, in isolated cases, killed their officers. Almost 750,000 French soldiers were involved in the mutiny. Not even the removal of General Nivelle and some of his subordinates ended the disaffection.

One regiment of young soldiers heading for the front kept "baa-ing" like sheep to show they were being led to slaughter. When reprimanded by their colonel, the *poilus* turned around and marched back to camp still bleating like docile lambs.

All through France, discontent rumbled; munitions workers went on strike; coal miners paraded in thousands against the war; Paris was torn by antiwar rioting. For a time, the

French capital resembled a second Petrograd. But the doomsday bell had not yet tolled for France.

Enough loyal troops were found to hold the trenches against the Germans. Amazingly, despite their excellent intelligence service, the enemy remained ignorant of the great French Army mutiny. Rumors seeped through to the headquarters of the Crown Prince Rupprecht, commanding the German troops in the area most affected, but he discounted them.

"I would sooner believe the millenium was at hand than that Frenchmen are mutineers," the Crown Prince said.

With this attitude, Crown Prince Rupprecht threw away Germany's chance to win the war. A full-scale offensive against the demoralized French Army might have swept on to Paris and victory.

By the time Rupprecht learned all the facts it was too late. On May 15, Nivelle was replaced by the "Hero of Verdun," General Henri Philippe Pétain, whom the *poilus* trusted as a friend.

"The types like Nivelle, the glory-seekers, will climb to the top over our bodies, but not Pétain. He is a soldier's soldier," declared a front-line noncom.

A stern disciplinarian, Pétain ended the mutiny with firmness. He had 23 ringleaders shot by firing squads. Some 250 men, including many from the Russian brigades attached to the French, were brought to a quiet sector and annihilated by their own artillery. About 100 soldiers were sent to Devil's Island and other places of exile. Certain mutinous units were put in exposed front-line positions and decimated by the Germans. Thus, the mutiny was bloodily wiped out in accordance with old-fashioned military justice.

However, once the troublemakers had been dealt with, Pétain proved he deserved the confidence of the soldiers. He visited more than 100 divisions and talked to the men, promising there would be no more "useless bloodletting" such as they had known in the past.

"The day of bad generalship is over! I, Henri Philippe Pétain, tell you this! Soldiers! Together we will win the victory without an extra life being lost! I swear it!" Pétain promised the Army.

The general liberalized leaves, improved conditions in rest camps, provided recreational facilities behind the lines, improved the food and slowly nursed the French Army back to health.

Although griping still continued and Communists still agitated for peace, the soldiers lowered the red flag and turned their faces to the enemy. Civilians ended the strikes and France proceeded with the war.

However, the shaken French Army was fit only for defensive duty. The burden of attack fell on the British while the Allies waited for Americans to come in sufficient numbers to turn the tide. (After June, 1917, contingents of United States troops were reaching France at the rate of 50,000 per month.)

But the Americans were still far from ready for combat. Once again Tommy Atkins went slogging through the Flanders mud in another battle at Ypres. From June 7, 1917, when the British exploded a huge mine under the German positions on Messines Ridge, until the end of the year, the armies wallowed in Flanders. The landscape was "nightmarish . . . a huge, undrained bog . . . a quagmire of churned slime, where once the most fertile farms in Europe had flourished," an observer commented.

The British and Germans swayed back and forth in the mud, each with a death grip on the other's throat. Here, at Ypres in 1917, the Germans first used mustard gas, a blistering, burning chemical; and here, British fliers again beat the Germans in the air.

Fighting raged all over the world. In Palestine, an Arab revolt led by T. E. Lawrence against the Turks helped British General Sir Edmund Allenby capture Jerusalem, while in Persia, General Sir Stanley Maude ended the German vision of a Berlin-to-Baghdad railway by capturing that city of the Arabian Nights. Deep in East Africa, the British finally captured the last German stronghold, although the crafty German, General Paul von Lettow-Vorbeck, fought on.

The year 1917 ended with a British victory on the western front at Cambrai, where tanks were at last properly utilized and in sufficient numbers to be a serious factor. On November 20, General Julian Byng's Third Army, led by 324 tanks, attacked a section of the Hindenburg Line behind a thick smoke screen. The armor punched deep holes into the German front, and a great British triumph seemed to be in the making.

However, the vehicles eventually bogged down and the attack came to a halt after a four-mile gain in one day—more than had been made at Ypres in a hundred days. The lesson of Cambrai was not lost; the key to victory on the ground was tanks and more tanks, correctly employed and backed by masses of infantry reserves. Future Allied tactics were shaped at Cambrai. There, too, American participation assumed some proportions. More than 2,500 Yanks—engineers and medics—were engaged in the battle.

(The first time Americans had actually faced the enemy was near Nancy at 6:05 A.M., October 23, when men of the First Division, holding a quiet sector, fired at the Germans. In early November, three Yanks, the first of thousands, were killed by an enemy hand grenade, and the war came home to every American.)

4

"YOU'RE IN THE ARMY NOW!"

AMERICA ENTERED THE WAR WITH THE ENTHUSIAM AND
energy of youth. The nation flexed its muscles and pitched
into the job. Factories turning out war matériel worked
around the clock; steel-mill forge fires roared high; machines
and men toiled ceaselessly. "Uncle Sam's in it all the way!" a
war poster stated, and the country agreed.

The United States went onto a war basis almost overnight.
Everyone "did his bit," from housewives to schoolchildren.
There were meatless days and wheatless days, lightless days
and heatless days; butter, sugar, cooking fats and white bread
were rationed; the American housewife made do with left-
overs to conserve food.

Prices skyrocketed and within a few weeks after the United
States entry into the war the cost of living doubled. Tran-
quil, isolated America meandering along its own rambling
path was gone forever. The United States had stepped fully
upon the center stage of history.

No longer could Americans take for granted their good
fortune. The time had come when Americans would have
to fight to preserve their cherished "way of life."

So America went to war with exuberance and elation. For
three years, the conflict in Europe had been raging three
thousand miles away, but the average American still did
not quite realize that war was death, starvation and disease.

War still had a touch of glory and glamour, Americans thought. They soon learned better.

Few of them had ever been in combat. Aging Civil War verterans spun yarns about Shiloh and Gettysburg, Fredericksburg and Cold Harbor—but their memories were dim. Some Americans had served in the war with Spain, almost two decades earlier; and some had fought Filipino insurrectionists back in 1900 and 1901. But those former soldiers remembered tainted beef, yellow fever and malaria, rather than the bullets and the shells.

Except for the few gallant volunteers with the British and the French, no American had personal knowledge of modern warfare. Even the Regular Army officers were trained amateurs who had never put military theory into practice.

Never before had the United States tried to do so much so quickly. The clatter of hammers raised busy echoes as army cantonments and training camps were built on prairies and in forests with incredible speed. Shipyards came to teeming life. Workers swarmed over the skeleton hulls of new vessels. Merchantmen and warships slid down the ways in growing numbers. Everywhere one saw the activities of a nation girding for war. Boy Scouts collected scrap iron and metal junk; children bought war savings stamps, and their parents subscribed to the Liberty Loan.

For the first time at the beginning of a war, the United States government resorted to the conscription of men for the Army (the Navy, requiring fewer men, still sought volunteers.) A draft law was passed on May 19, 1917. It required all American males between the ages of twenty-one and thirty to register on June 5, 1917, for possible military duty.

Wilson took this step reluctantly. In the past, the American Army had been filled by volunteers, but the President and Congress realized that an army of several millions could not be raised that way. Once before, the United States had enacted a conscription bill. That was in 1863, during the Civil War. The result had been a catastrophe. Violent riots erupted against the draft in New York City. Mobs ran wild for nearly a week, burning, killing and looting. Troops rushed from the fighting front had finally quelled the rioters.

Because conscription smacked of autocracy and tyranny, Americans detested it. Besides, more than 13 per cent of the American people came from German background; an equal number had their ancestral origins in the Austro-Hungarian Empire. No man could foretell whether such people would willingly register for a draft that might force them to go as soldiers against their own kinsmen.

Speaking of the draft law, Senator James A. Reed warned Secretary of War Newton D. Baker, "You will have the streets of our cities running red with blood on draft registration day."

The senator's grim prophecy remained unfulfilled. On Tuesday, June 5, 1917, a day balmy with the touch of approaching summer, nearly ten million young Americans went lightheartedly to designated places and registered for the draft.

"They came from everywhere . . . cities, towns and hamlets . . . shoe clerks, cowboys, students, farmers . . . an outpouring of American manhood answered the call and Uncle Sam was proud of his nephews," wrote a New York *Journal* reporter in a feature article about registration day

Once the men had been registered, the drafting process began. On July 20, 1917, at 9:49 A.M., Secretary of War Newton D. Baker stood blindfolded before a large bowl containing 10,500 black capsules with numbered slips inside them.

The numbers in the capsules matched names entered on registration lists in each of 4,500 local draft boards. The registrants had been listed serially beginning with number one. There were 10,500 capsules, since that was the largest number listed by any draft board.

Secretary Baker reached into the bowl and drew out a capsule. The number was 258. (In the World War II draft the first number drawn was 158.) By telephone, ticker and telegraph, the news sped to all local draft boards that men bearing the number 258 had been tapped for the Army and would become soldiers if they passed physical tests.

The lottery continued until 2:00 A.M. July 21, when 10,500 numbers were finally drawn. The ponderous draft machinery rolled into motion. By late fall, more than 516,000 men filled the training camps. Less than a year later some 2,500,-000 young Americans wore a uniform; and for them and those to follow, life would never again be quite the same. By 1919 more than 4,000,000 Americans had seen some army service, while another 800,000 went into the Navy.

"You're in the Army now!" sang the draftees, "You're not behind the plow!" They came from all walks of life and took private's pay—$21.00 per month—through a rigorous basic training period of ten weeks during which they learned to be soldiers.

Because not enough camps were ready for the floods of recruits, men drilled in city parks—ball fields became parade grounds and the "Hup! Two! Three! Four!" of the drill sergeants rose above the street traffic.

The draftees worked hard and before long discovered, to their own surprise, that they were cavalrymen, artillerymen and infantrymen, who thought, talked and behaved like soldiers—not civilians. The transformation was miraculous; few believed that independent, undisciplined Americans could so quickly be turned into soldiers.

The Allies felt that a token force of Americans would bolster the morale of their people, and Wilson responded at once.

The 1st U.S. Infantry Division was formed from various Regular Army units, and its advance echelon sailed to England and France, led by Black Jack Pershing, who had been promoted to major general and given command of the American Expeditionary Force (A.E.F.). Attached to the 1st Division was a regiment of U.S. Marines. The arrival of the Americans touched off demonstrations in London and Paris. The French were especially cordial to the Yanks.

At a welcoming ceremony near Paris, Pershing won instant popularity when he responded to a welcoming speech by the new French Premier, Georges Clemenceau, who once had practiced medicine in Greenwich Village, New York.

Clemenceau, known as "The Tiger," spoke eloquently as he thanked the Americans for coming to France's aid. To this Pershing replied, "We are merely repaying a debt of long standing." He then squared his shoulders and exclaimed, in careful French, *"Nous voilà, Lafayette!"* (We are here, Lafayette!) A roar went up from his listeners. Black Jack had pressed the key to French hearts.

From June on, more and still more American troops poured into France and Britain through a half-dozen Atlantic ports. The rest of the 1st Division, advance elements of the 2nd, 26th, 42nd (Rainbow) and several Marine regiments came tramping off the transports.

Pershing set up his headquarters at Chaumont. American supply dumps and bases were established all over France, and the doughboys went into serious combat training. General Pershing also showed the Allies another side of his nature—a stubborn streak.

Both Haig and Pétain tried to persuade him that American troops should be incorporated with the British and French armies. Later, when Marshal Ferdinand Foch was appointed supreme commander of Allied Forces, he also suggested the Yanks be used as replacements under British and French commanders.

Pershing made his position clear. "We shall fight as Americans in an American army under the American flag and American command!" And that was that!

While the A.E.F. took advanced combat training, the United States Navy was already in action on the submarine-infested Atlantic, where the Germans were winning the U-boat war. The first United States ships to take up war duty—six destroyers led by Captain J. K. Taussig—arrived at Queenstown, Ireland, a key transatlantic base, on May 4, 1917.

Taussig reported for duty to a British admiral who asked, "How many days will you require to make ready for sea?"

"I shall be ready when refueled, sir!" Taussig replied.

In this spirit, the United States Navy joined the cruel war at sea against the submarines.

It was a war of craft, skill and courage, a war of endurance and sacrifice. American warships escorted the merchant convoys, attacked subs, laid mines and patrolled the Dover Straits against German surface raiders.

The scales of the ocean war swung slowly against Germany as new Allied antisubmarine tactics began taking a growing toll of U-boats.

At the same time, the entry of the United States Navy into the war created an atmosphere of gloom and defeatism throughout the immobilized German and Austrian navies.

At the beginning of 1917, Austrian sailors briefly mutinied at the Adriatic naval base of Cattaro. Red flags were raised to the mainmasts of several cruisers. Harsh measures quickly stamped out the fires of revolt, but the sparks still smoldered.

A riot broke out aboard several ships of the Kaiser's fleet, late in May. Again red flags flew and Communist slogans were shouted. Again, the insurrection was quickly crushed.

Soon after, trouble occurred on the German cruisers *Printz-regent Leopold* and *Friedrich der Grosse.* Sailors on both ships refused to obey orders. Two ringleaders were executed, and the mutinous men returned to duty; but demoralization had taken hold and was eating away the once-proud German Navy.

If the Kaiser's sailors sulked and brooded, the German people also grew restive. Despite all the costly victories on land, despite all the U-boat victories at sea, the war was not yet won. On every German street, blind, maimed and mutilated soldiers dragged along on crutches and canes in an endless procession of misery brought on by Kaiser Wilhelm's ambitions.

"Germany is mourning her fallen sons . . ." wrote a Swedish reporter. ". . . Everywhere one sees tear-stained faces and red-rimmed eyes. . . . All Germany is weeping."

There was not only sorrow in Germany, but hunger as well. The British blockade was unbroken despite the submarines, and 1917 became the "starving time."

The once sleek and portly German burghers and their plump *frauen* were now thin and wasted. Children went to bed hungry. Underfed factory workers collapsed at their machines.

Germans who had glutted themselves on fowl, steaks and roasts now existed on boiled turnip greens and *ersatz* bread. Conditions were even worse in Austria. Gay Vienna was "a morgue, a tomb of living despair," according to one observer. The Hungarians, too, ate meagerly and dressed in threadbare clothing. All of Germany's allies suffered want and lived in misery. The war which Kaiser Wilhelm and Emperor Franz Josef had launched now hovered like a bird of doom.

5

THE INTELLECTUAL WARRIOR

THE ONLY WARFARE FOR WHICH THE GERMANS WERE TOTALLY unprepared was the kind Woodrow Wilson waged—a war of ideas and ideals. Wilson understood that the world conflict could not be won by planes, tanks, guns, ships and soldiers alone. Some greater force was necessary: a dynamic cause, a vital purpose. Physical victory was not enough for Wilson; he needed moral triumph as well.

"It would be a crime against humanity to win the war and lose the peace," Wilson said. "We must have noble aims and aspirations so that no mother will feel her son has died in vain."

Until the entry of the United States, all the big powers had gone to war for selfish reasons. Each stood to gain from the hostilities. Greed, power and ambition had impelled the Kaiser and his cohorts to start the war.

The French, British and Russians had marched to thwart him. Thus the war was a struggle to dominate Europe and world markets. Rising Germany wanted the British and French colonial empires, and those countries were fighting to keep the status quo.

The Germans could cope with enemies such as Britain, France and Russia. One resorted to trickery, strategems and wily diplomacy to gain one's ends. When peaceful ways failed, one made war if the moment was right and the chances for victory high. The great war then raging had been an outgrowth of this age-old pattern; but the makers of the war had reaped a whirlwind. The destructive new weapons had added previously unthinkable horrors to war: poison gas, the airplane, the tank, liquid flame throwers, high-explosive shells, the U-boat and the magnetic mine.

The warmongers also had opened a Pandora's box of social storm. The 1917 Russian Revolution shook the monarchies of Europe. If kings and emperors trembled at the fluttering red flags in Russia, the war-weary masses saw bright hope in those same banners.

Despite the storms of change sweeping through Europe and reaching to the remote corners of the earth, shortsighted men fed the fires of the war and groped through smoke and flames, blindly hanging on to the shabby belief that once the war was won, everything would return to the familiar ways of the past.

And because they clung to hoary ideas—colonialism, imperialism, power blocs, secret alliances and disregard of national minorities—whether the Allies or Germany won, unborn generations were condemned to doom in other wars, for the cancer that caused the tragedy of 1914 had not been cut out.

President Wilson wanted to change all this. He was determined that this would be the last war. In America, the Germans faced a different sort of enemy, one whose President raised the slogan "The War to end all War!" and vowed that his country was dedicated to "the liberation of all peoples, the Germans included."

Never before had the Germans fought a foe who preached war without hate and held out to mankind the concept of perpetual peace to be won through a League of Nations, many countries banded together in a "concert of peace."

If Wilson bewildered the Germans, he also confused

England and France. The leaders of those nations, realists such as Lloyd George and Georges Clemenceau, had baldly stated their war aim: to crush Germany so she could never rise again.

Now, the head of their newest and most powerful partner was saying the war must have higher purposes than victory in the field. Wilson's declarations embarrassed the Allied leaders. They had to agree with him or else suffer public disapproval for not backing a peaceful future.

Wilson tried to drive a wedge between the Kaiser and his subjects. He stressed over and over that the United States "has no quarrel with the German people. . . . We have no feelings towards them but one of sympathy and friendship."

At first, his words did little to turn the Germans away from the Kaiser. But, in 1918, as the war's grist mill continued its demands on the Germans, Wilson's speeches, printed as leaflets and dropped by plane over Germany, became beacons in the war-clouded darkness.

On January 8, 1918, Wilson (the "Intellectual Warrior," a newspaper columnist dubbed him) delivered a speech before Congress outlining the war aims and peace terms of the United States.

In this talk, Wilson listed Fourteen Points for a lasting peace not only in Europe but also throughout the whole world. One point or another appealed to every existing nation and to all the minorities who hoped for freedom and independence.

The Fourteen Points stressed freedom of the seas; gave assurance to Russia that her form of government would be allowed to flourish without interference; promised autonomy to the peoples of the Austro-Hungarian Empire and all other minorities; and most important, guaranteed that no secret deals were to be made around the peace table.

"Open covenants, openly arrived at . . ." was the first of the Fourteen Points.

Wilson wove a splendid tapestry of the postwar world for the war-weary and oppressed masses. His Fourteen Points served to bolster the fighting men of the Allied armies, navies and air forces; he made them feel that they were crusaders in a glorious cause, not merely the cannon fodder of another imperialistic war.

Despite the impact of the Fourteen Points, the Germans did not yield. They still hoped to win the victory by a last, tremendous military blow that would force the Allies to surrender before the full weight of the United States' might could be brought to bear.

A short time after, Wilson added Four Points to the original Fourteen. The Four Points he described as ". . . the ends for which the associated peoples of the world are fighting and which must be conceded before there is peace."

The first point called for an end to autocracy everywhere; the second restated the rights of all peoples to self-determination; the third expressed hope for civilized relationships among various nations; and the fourth stressed the need for a League of Nations.

The American President appealed directly to the Germans, calling upon them to get rid of the Kaiser and the military autocrats who ruled them. In return, Wilson promised them a peace treaty in which "There shall be no annexation, no contributions, no punitive damages. . . ."

In his zeal, President Wilson acted as though he spoke for all the Allied powers. Neither Great Britain nor France had ever promised peace terms without annexations, contributions or punitive damages. On the contrary, Clemenceau and Lloyd George meant to force harsh terms on Germany.

However, both these leaders offered no objections to

Wilson's peace terms. Georges Clemenceau smiled whenever the President's "equitable peace" was mentioned.

The Tiger (who had been so named for his political fierceness) reputedly said, "Mr. Wilson is a humanitarian. No one can find fault with his proposals for a humane peace. I submit, however, that the war is far from over; the *boches* are still undefeated. Grievous times will beset us before the enemy falls. I suggest that Mr. Wilson think about winning the war and letting the peace take care of itself."

A British official stated: "The American President speaks of peace without revenge. Well he may. He has not been fighting the Hun these years; he has not seen his countrymen torn and bleeding. I believe Mr. Wilson's lofty sentiments will vanish when American blood is spilled."

Although Allied leaders responded cynically to Wilson, the plain people of Europe saw him as a Messiah come to guide them out of war's hell. His picture hung on walls in the humble homes of Italian peasants, Serbian goatherds, Breton fishermen and Yorkshire farmers. Everywhere, the man in the street worshipped Wilson.

In Germany, men wondered why the war had to continue. And they wondered, too, if *Herr* Wilson might not be telling the truth. If, as *Herr* Wilson had said, the Americans did not wish to make war on the German people, then only the Kaiser stood in the way of peace. Early in the year 1918, the full meaning of Wilson's Fourteen Points and his Four Points drifted into German consciousness and a tremor of revolt convulsed that unhappy land.

Slogans were painted on factory walls: "Out with the Kaiser!" "We Want Peace!" "Down With the War!" Those demands appeared in Berlin and Essen, in Hamburg and Cologne, in all the cities of Germany. Mysterious fires and sabotage of war plants took place throughout Germany and the clamor for peace grew louder.

The Kaiser was not yet through. His efficient secret agents rounded up the saboteurs and defeatists; Communists, Socialists and peace advocates were arrested. Firing squads were busy for a while, and the voices of dissent fell temporarily silent.

Then, the German war machine, like a dying beast, gathered its strength in March, 1918, for one last, ultimate effort.

6

"WITH OUR BACKS TO THE WALL . . ."

AT ABOUT 10:00 A.M., MARCH 26, 1918, AN EXPLOSION ROCKED a Paris shopping street, killing a few people and wounding scores. Air raid sirens wailed out a warning, and the crowds scurried to shelter.

Antiaircraft gunners scanned the skies for the raiders. Swift Nieuport chasers went up to engage the enemy, but found no hostile planes.

A few minutes later another blast wrecked some buildings and caused more casualties. A series of such detonations followed, and all Paris verged on panic as rumors winged through the city.

"The *boches* have planes covered with paint that makes them invisible!' went one story.

Similar tales circulated about the city until the residents were nearly frantic. The truth about the mysterious explosions was scarcely less fantastic than the most incredible yarns.

It was discovered that the Germans were shelling Paris from emplacements seventy-five miles away with a monster cannon they called "Big Bertha," named for the wife of munitions manufacturer Alfred Krupp, who had made the gun.

"Big Bertha" further weakened French civilian morale, for she had come onstage at a time when the war was at its most critical point for France since 1914.

On March 21, along a forty-mile-wide front at the Somme

River, seventy-one German divisions under General Erich Ludendorff attacked the twenty-six British divisions guarding the sector between La Bassée and La Fère. In the foggy dawn that first spring day of 1918, a tremendous barrage of gas and high explosives shattered British artillery and rocked the men in trenches. The massive German effort to end the war had begun. Ludendorff planned to crash through the undermanned British front, turn north to the sea and push Haig's armies into the Channel.

The German general came close to succeeding in the bloody struggle known as the Second Battle of the Somme. Ludendorff was helped by British internal political squabbling. Prime Minister Lloyd George, determined to keep General Haig from repeating the costly offensive of 1917, insisted upon retaining in England a large force of troops which he refused to release unless the plans for using them were approved by the cabinet.

As a result, Haig had few reserves in France. His available divisions were stretched thin when the big German onslaught came. Ludendorff's troops gained fourteen miles in four days—the greatest advance on the western front in almost four years.

Under the stresses of the emergency, General Haig and General Pétain, the French commander, argued over strategy, tactics, troop movements and reinforcements. Conflicting orders were issued and confusion spread among the forces trying to check Ludendorff.

However, the differences between Haig and Pétain brought an unexpected dividend when General (later Marshal) Ferdinand Foch was appointed on March 26 as coordinator of the Franco-British armies on the western front. A week later, April 8, he became commander-in-chief of all Allied forces in France.

Ludendorff's advance threatened the vital rail center of

Amiens, and only a heroic stand by the British stopped him just short of his goal. By April 5, the Second Battle of the Somme flickered to an end.

The gasping Allies stood in dazed wonder that they had been able to halt the foe. It was a costly feat: the British lost 160,000 men, including 90,000 prisoners. The French losses were almost 70,000. German casualties, never accurately tabulated, totaled close to 100,000 killed, wounded and missing. Although Ludendorff failed to take Amiens, his troops had reached a point only seven miles from the city, capturing tons of military supplies and many guns, besides forcing Haig to commit almost all his reserves.

The Germans correctly regarded the Second Battle of the Somme as a victory. But, unknown to Ludendorff, his superior, General Paul von Hindenburg, the Kaiser or the German people, that triumph, which set bells ringing across the Fatherland, only served to make inevitable Germany's doom.

After nearly four years of fruitless attempts to establish a unified Allied command on the western front, the German success at the Somme forced the proper decision. From April 8 until the end of the war, Marshal Foch would coordinate the efforts of the British, French and American armies until a day, eight months in the future, when the bugles signaled "Cease-fire!" and the long war would be at an end. But during the early weeks of spring, no man could foretell what lay ahead. The way seemed dark and hopeless for the Allies.

"No matter how hard we fight, the Germans always come back stronger. For the first time, one hears defeatist talk in London. This is most disheartening; if the average Englishman, with all his tenacity, feels whipped, I say we've had it!" a British infantry officer home on leave after the Second Battle of the Somme, wrote a friend at the front.

Pessimism spread across Britain and France; and even brash America stood in worried doubt during April, 1918. That month, early flowers blossomed in ravaged Flanders and green shoots appeared in devastated Picardy. Spring had come to the wasteland of war. The uneasy silence of dormant battlegrounds was broken by warbling birds back from their winter's migration.

The troubled Allied generals wondered where the next German blow would fall. They had not long to wait. On April 9, Ludendorff struck another sledgehammer blow at Lys, just south of Ypres. This onslaught, officially known as the Battle of Lys, or the Third Battle of Ypres, lasted three weeks until April 30. The German objective was Hazebrouck, an important rail junction. Once that had been gained, Ludendorff intended to reach the Channel coast thus isolating the British armies from the French.

Most of Haig's divisions had been badly mauled at the Somme and were greatly understrength when Ludendorff attacked. The Germans gained swift initial successes. A Portuguese division, directly in the path of the *Reichswehr* attack, was decimated.

By April 12, Haig's last reserves had been committed and German advance patrols entered the outskirts of Hazebrouck. That day, Haig sent a ringing order to his embattled soldiers:

> There is no other course open to us but to fight it out. Every position must be held to the last man. . . . With our backs to the wall and believing in the justice of our cause each one must fight on to the end.

Haig called for help from the Royal Flying Corps. British planes bombed and strafed the advancing Germans. The airmen fought thrilling duels a mile above the ground. Again

British fliers proved superior, but they could not stop the German advance.

The old battleground at Ypres flared up once more. Despite a valiant stand by Haig's men, the Germans took Messines Ridge where, it was said, a British soldier had given his life for each yard. From Ypres to the coastal flatlands, tens of thousands were locked in combat. At last, bolstered by seven reserve French divisions, the British stemmed the German flood and the Third Battle of Ypres ended on April 30.

The Allies lost some 350,000 men in six weeks; the Germans not many less. Casualties had drained British strength to the bone. Several divisions had been whittled down to scarcely more than regiments in size. Some units were totally annihilated. Replacements rushed to Haig from England, Palestine, Africa, Mesopotamia and Macedonia; but until they arrived, British armies in France could do no more than barely hold their positions.

The front remained quiet for several weeks after Third Ypres. Ludendorff needed a breathing spell and wanted time to regroup for another thrust. But the sands were running out for German opportunities on the western front. General Pershing's American Expeditionary Force (A.E.F.) was nearly ready for full-scale combat operations.

German propagandists had derided American fighting ability; and the Allies, too, expressed doubt that Pershing could manage a battle mission with his hastily trained troops.

Black Jack Pershing had faith in his doughboys. "They are the sons of a nation that has never lost a war," he said. "When the zero hour comes, these Americans will not fail to carry on the traditions of Bunker Hill, Gettysburg and San Juan."

The 1st Division, A.E.F., which had a hard core of well-disciplined regulars, shaped up well in advanced combat training. During the first week of May, Pershing felt the unit was ready for a test in battle.

He persuaded Marshal Foch to let the division carry out a limited offensive operation; the troops had been defending the trenches in a quiet sector for several weeks. Foch agreed and gave the 1st Division the task of capturing Cantigny, a strongly fortified German-held village near Amiens. A French tank unit was sent to support the attack.

The 1st Division doughboys moved into position around Cantigny on May 27, and the attack was scheduled to start at 4:00 A.M. the following day behind a rolling barrage from massed divisional artillery. (The guns were French 75-mm. howitzers. American-made artillery had not yet arrived in any great quantities.)

The eastern sky was tinted pink at 4:00 A.M., May 28. Morning breezes were gentle but cool. Delicate wild flowers blossomed in the shell-torn fields that stretched from the American lines to shattered Cantigny. Sleepy doughboys staring across the tortured land could discern, in the growing light, the charred skeletons of ruined cottages and farm buildings. Somewhere, across that No Man's Land, hidden in the ruin and rubble, were the Germans. Seasoned veterans from the eastern front defended Cantigny, men who had spent almost four years in combat against the Russians.

They had grown accustomed to winning, and untried Americans posed no threat to them. The Germans stirred lazily in the dawning day. At 4:00 A.M. squads lined up at field kitchens for breakfast: hot porridge, thick chunks of *ersatz* bread and a steaming liquid that resembled coffee but tasted like "boiled bilge water."

That meal was never served. From the distance there came the jarring blast of massed cannon. Seconds later, shells began exploding on the German positions. Men dropped their mess tins and dove for cover. The shelling was rapid and accurate.

"The guns were served by expert artillerymen," a German soldier recalled. "Seldom had we faced such a bombardment. You couldn't lift your head out of the dirt. The air was filled with shrapnel and flying debris."

The men at the guns were far from expert; they were green Yanks firing their maiden combat mission. The "redlegs" (the nickname for U.S. artillerymen) went to work with an ardor that made up for their lack of experience.

The barrage pounded the Germans for almost an hour before the doughboys went "over the top" for the first time in the war. They advanced in widespread ranks, running at a crouch. Ahead waddled the tanks. Anxious officers watched the attack through field glasses.

"No one knew how the boys would act under fire," a regimental commander said. "Green troops are usually unreliable, but not those First Division lads. They went on like tried veterans and never even flinched when the Heinie machine guns opened up."

Germans fire was not enough to stop the Yanks that day. They swept irresistibly forward with bayonet and hand grenades, wiping out machine-gun nests and storming German positions. Straight into Cantigny they poured. After a brief swirl of hand-to-hand fighting, the enemy fled. Several hundred Germans surrendered, and elated doughboys prodded their crestfallen prisoners back across no man's land.

American rifles and machine guns routed a German counterattack; the day ended with Cantigny firmly in American hands. The A.E.F. had vindicated Pershing's demand for a separate American army and the victory gave a tremendous boost to Allied morale.

It was about the only good news the Allies heard that last

week in May. On the twenty-seventh, the day before the battle of Cantigny, Ludendorff threw another powerhouse punch at the Allies. The German general knew the Allies had suffered more than 350,000 casualties since March 26. Although his own losses were about equal, numerical superiority still rested with him.

His next assault fell on the French. He thrust at them with forty-two divisions on a twenty-five-mile-wide front in the Chemin des Dames sector. That hard-won ground was wrested from the *poilus* in the first day of what was called the Third Battle of the Aisne.

While the Americans were fighting at Cantigny, the Germans crossed the Aisne River and thrust a deep salient into the French lines. By June 2–3, German scout cars were in Château-Thierry on the Marne River, fifty-six miles from Paris.

In this crisis, Marshal Foch sent a call for help to General Pershing. Black Jack rushed the raw 2nd and 3rd Divisions to the Marne near Château-Thierry. Now the world would learn whether the Americans had the heart for large-scale modern warfare; compared to what was coming, Cantigny had been a skirmish.

7

THE ELEVENTH HOUR

THE PRUSSIAN GUARDS WERE THE PICKED TROOPS OF THE GER-
man Army. This elite regiment had never met defeat in
battle. Each man stood six feet tall and had been selected for
skill and courage. No other regiment could boast so many
decorations for bravery in action.

Ludendorff gave the Guards the honor of leading the assault across the Marne River at Château-Thierry. The
crossings began June 3. The Guardsmen forded the stream
at several points, splashing through the waist-deep water like
automatons. Some reached the south bank before running
into resistance. That day, the best German soldiers met the
finest Americans. A brigade of U.S. Marines, attached to the
2nd Infantry Division, was holding the line where the
crossings were attempted.

The Marines attacked with such fury that the Prussian
Guards nicknamed them *teuffelhunten*—"Devil Dogs." The
Leathernecks were more than a match for the Guardsmen.
Never before had the Germans faced such fighters.

"The Yankees were madmen. They rushed down upon
us like wild Indians, with blood-curdling shrieks. They
were mad—but magnificent," a German officer wrote after
the war.

The U.S. Marines, the tough, sun-baked Leathernecks

who had fought "from the Halls of Montezuma to the shores of Tripoli" now added Château-Thierry to their battle streamers.

For almost the first time in the war, Prussian Guardsmen turned tail and ran. The battle around Château-Thierry lasted until June 6, and when it was over, the U.S. Marines held the pulverized ruins of the village.

Puzzled and angry, the Germans pulled back to re-estimate the Americans. The newcomers could fight; that the Germans no longer doubted. They were well equipped and well fed. Tremors of doubt crept into the minds of German soldiers; they had been told by their leaders that no Americans would ever reach France—the U-boats would see to that.

But the Americans were there. Now the Germans saw they had been deceived. Even the Kaiser had lied to them. Hopelessness sapped the spirit of German troops. They still fought with valor and tenacity, but knew that a German victory was only a fading dream.

Again and yet again, Ludendorff tried to break through, and the Marne River again became a German graveyard. The Kaiser's armies were played out by mid-July. Food shortages reached the critical point inside Germany—the barest necessities were almost nonexistent; hunger was commonplace; famine and disease threatened. Socialist and Communist agitators called on the German masses to revolt. "Let us follow the example of our Russian brothers!" cried Karl Liebknecht, a leading Communist. "Down with the Kaiser!"

The workers in steel mills, munitions plants and factories heeded Liebknecht. They struck by the thousands, and every day in German cities special riot police clashed with demonstrators who demanded immediate peace and the Kaiser's abdication.

Germany's allies, too, were breaking under the strain.

Turkey and Bulgaria teetered on chaos and ruin; the Austro-Hungarian Empire had the death rattle in its throat.

Conversely, in Great Britain, France and the United States, in all the countries at war with Germany, there rose a sense of elation. The German threat had been broken on the Marne, and though the enemy had inflicted almost one million casualties in his last struggles, the Allies still had strength and resources. The moment to strike back had arrived.

On July 18, Marshal Foch ordered French, British and American troops to attack all along the western front. It was a gigantic offensive involving millions of men. As the infantry pressed forward, swarms of Allied warplanes brought retribution down upon the Germans with bombs, bullets and incendiaries. Slowly at first, then rapidly, the enemy pulled back across the scarred and pitted battlegrounds where so many had fallen in four years of bloodletting.

During the early days of August, the discipline of some German units fell apart; deserters crossed into Allied lines and prisoners gave up without a struggle. By August 14, members of the German General Staff suggested that a favorable opportunity should be found to make peace.

But the fighting went on and on. Summer passed. Bulgaria surrendered unconditionally on September 29. A month later, Turkey gave up. Austria still remained in the arena, but not for long; by November 3, that country also capitulated.

Meanwhile, awful battles blazed in France and Belgium; some of the war's worst fighting took place as the Americans pushed through Belleau Wood and the Argonne Forest. The Germans fell back on the Hindenburg Line. But as September waned, Ludendorff advised Hindenburg that further resistance was senseless; in his opinion an armistice should be sought.

On October 4, a new German chancellor, Prince Max of

Champagne and the Argonne

Vauquois
Bourreuilles
Bois des Bel Orme
Argonne
Bois de Fontaine Madame
Bois de la Chalade
La Fille Morte
Clermont
Les Islettes
Ste-Menehould
Grand Pré
Vouziers
R. Dormoise
R. Aisne
Cernay
Binarville
Bois de Grurie
Vienne-le-Four de Paris
Château
Bois des Hauts Batis
Chausson
Le Mesnil
Vienne-la-Ville
Vienne-le-Villé
Valmy
Tahure
Butte de Tahure
Maison de Champagne (191)
The Bastion
Massiges
Beauséjour
R. Tourbe
To Mézières
B. de Souain
Somme-Py
Navarin Farm
Épine de Videgrange
Maison de Mesnil
La Baraque
Trou Bricot
Bois Sabot
Mesnil
Perthes Road
Suippes
Souain
Camp de Châlons
Auberive
R. Verle
Châlons-sur-Marne
R. Suippe
To Rethel & Mézières
Bazancourt
Nogent-l'Abbesse
Pompelle Hill
Verzy
Canal
R. Marne
Prunay
RHEIMS
Silery
Betheny
B-mont
Ay
Tunnel
Marne Canal

Miles
0 5 10 15 20 25 30

Baden, contacted President Wilson through the Swiss embassy in Washington and asked for an armistice on the basis of the Fourteen Points. Wilson curtly informed him that he should contact Marshal Foch for surrender terms.

The Intellectual Warrior wanted the war to end as soon as possible, but firmly declared that it had to be a military victory on conditions negotiated between soldiers, not politicians; the place for the statesmen was around the peace conference table, not on the battlefield.

In October, the Hindenburg Line was smashed wide open, and with American troops leading the way, a pell-mell race began toward the German border.

All at once, during the last week of that crucial month, the volcano erupted inside Germany. The High Seas Fleet broke out in full-scale mutiny, and revolutionary activity exploded throughout the *Reichswehr.* Ludendorff resigned on October 27, and the Army began to fall apart.

Rioting and street-fighting flared in Berlin between monarchists and left-wingers. Army units joined the radicals; red flags burgeoned over the German capital; brother fought brother in a vicious civil war as the Kaiser clung to his precarious throne.

By November 9, Wilhelm II realized that all was lost. He gave up the crown and fled to Holland the next day, leaving behind a defeated Fatherland torn by internal strife.

On the same day that the Kaiser gave up his throne, New York, Paris, Rome and London ran wild with joyous celebrations when the signing of an armistice was falsely reported by a correspondent of the United Press. The pent-up feelings of millions were loosed. Snake-dancing crowds rushed through the streets screaming in a dozen languages that the war was over.

But the elation was premature. The First World War went

on two days longer, during which men died. The idiocy had not yet run its full course.

A Socialist, Friedrich Ebert, took up the reins of a German government on the verge of anarchy. His request for an armistice was granted by Foch. At 5:00 A.M., November 11, 1918, in a railway car standing on a spur line inside the Forest of Compiègne, German representatives met Allied officers and signed an armistice calling for hostilities to cease at 11:00 A.M. that same day.

The war did not end at once; it grumbled and growled to its close along the thousand miles of trenches that ran across the Continent from the North Sea to the Swiss border. High in the Italian Alps, in woodlands and pastures, in broken cities and destroyed villages, wherever men had been fighting, an unaccustomed silence settled down.

The war was really over! Once more, crowds danced in London streets and on Paris boulevards; across the United States wild celebrations blocked traffic. Pandemonium gripped the people of the Allied world—the war was over!

The fighting men at the front showed no jubilation, only relief. They came out of the trenches and dugouts and stood in the pale November sunshine, gazing up at the sky with wary eyes. They moved about cautiously; the habits learned in combat were not so easily shed. But at last even the front-line troops accepted the truth that a man could walk erect without fear.

Now that the war had been brought to a conclusion, the struggle for a lasting peace started. The soldiers gave way to the diplomats, and a new contest began. Woodrow Wilson sailed to Europe as the head of the United States peace delegation; he was hailed by milling, shouting throngs wherever he went.

But Wilson's idealism, his Fourteen Points and Four

Points as well, were lost in a morass of distrust, suspicion and lingering hatred. England, France and Italy, represented by Lloyd George, Georges Clemenceau and Vittorio Orlando, wanted vengeance—too many English boys had fallen; too many Frenchmen and Italians had given their lives for justice to be tempered with mercy. The path of wreckage and rubble created by the Germans had left too much bitterness.

The Russian Revolution, now a violent civil war, raised the threat of Bolshevism in Europe. Soviet-type governments controlled by Communists reigned briefly in Bavaria (December, 1918–February, 1919). From March to August, 1919, the Communists ruled Hungary, and a Red army nearly captured Warsaw.

The fear of communism caused the Allies to support anti-Bolshevik forces. American, French, British, Czech and Japanese troops fought Reds in northern Russia and Siberia around Murmansk and Vladivostok. Not until April, 1920, did the more than ten thousand Yanks come home from an abortive expedition into Siberia, where young American soldiers died in battle long after the Armistice.

The statesmen talked peace, but there was no peace. In June, 1919, a reluctant Germany signed the Treaty of Versailles, embittered by terms which saddled future generations with staggering financial burdens to pay the cost of the war.

A German republic was created along democratic lines, but still nurtured the festering core of the old order and the seeds of an new one which would yet bring about another Armageddon. The world seethed and heaved with turmoil in the aftermath of the Great War. Yugoslavia and Czechoslovakia were hacked out of the Austro-Hungarian Empire; an independent Poland arose, and the Baltic states (Estonia, Latvia and Lithuania) came into being.

But changed boundary lines only created fresh problems,

Europe, after the War

while rancor still gnawed at men's hearts. The Treaty of Versailles solved nothing, nor did it "make the world safe for democracy" as Wilson had envisioned.

The Versailles Treaty did provide machinery for settling all future international disputes by creating the League of Nations. This body consisted of four main sections—the League of Nations Council, the League of Nations Assembly, the Permanent Court of International Justice and the League of Nations Secretariat. Headquarters of the League were at Geneva, Switzerland.

Membership in the League of Nations was mandatory for all nations signing the Versailles Treaty. This meant that the major powers of Europe and Asia belonged to it; the only big nation that failed to join was the United States, and that exception throttled the League of Nations at its birth.

After the Armistice, a wave of isolationism swept America, and the country turned against the internationalist policies of Woodrow Wilson. The President fought hard to make the United States a partner in the family of nations, but the people refused to heed him.

"Let Europe solve its own problems! We've had enough!" was the American attitude. The United States was enjoying an unequalled era of prosperity and well-being. People wanted to forget war and past crises. More than 100,000 Yanks had died and 243,000 suffered wounds to help end Europe's conflict. Now Americans wanted only to be left alone.

Woodrow Wilson pleaded and argued until a paralytic stroke felled him and his voice was stilled. The United States never entered the League of Nations, and that body floundered in hopeless irresolution while the drumbeats of dictatorships and war rose to a deafening crescendo.

In Italy, Benito Mussolini swaggered to power by 1922. That once unwarlike nation engaged in aggression against

Ethiopia and Albania. Fascist Blackshirt legions helped crush republican Spain. Across the Pacific, the Rising Sun flag of Imperial Japan was borne into Manchuria and China. But it remained for Germany to rise, like an evil phoenix, from the ruins of defeat, led by a fiendish genius, Adolf Hitler, who had been a corporal on the western front. Hitler came to power in 1933 on the heels of the depression when poverty, despair and disaster faced Germany.

Hitler scrapped the Versailles Treaty and rebuilt the German armed forces into a war machine unlike any the world had ever before seen. He flouted and mocked the democracies until, in 1939, Germany invaded Poland, and the Second World War broke out.

The heritage of World War I was World War II, far deadlier, far more brutal and destructive. It was the price the world had to pay for failing to build the foundations of a lasting peace through an international organization with the strength to enforce its mandates.

The impotent League of Nations was finally dissolved in 1946 when the United Nations held its first meeting. Symbolically, the gavel wielded by Trygve Lie, first Secretary General of the United Nations, was the one used at the final session of the old League.

The world now had the lessons of two ghastly wars; and this time the United States did not shun the international organization, but was one of its prime architects.

In the years since World War II, the United Nations has shown strength and weaknesses. There has been bloodshed in many parts of the globe—in Israel and Korea, in Egypt and Laos, in Algeria, the Congo and Vietnam—but the fires of war have not spread, because the United Nations stamped them out.

This period in history is a perilous one; two mighty economic and social systems—capitalism and communism—

are locked in a relentless struggle for supremacy. In 1914 and 1939, political differences brought on two world wars; today, when mankind can be wiped out by pushing a button, even the most ruthless and ambitious tyrants must give deep thought to the consequences of yet another global war.

Since the end of the Second World War, the United Nations has been both shield and bulwark in the struggle for peace. Perhaps, in this era of weapons able to destroy all civilization, even the most ruthless aggressor will shrink from another world war. For no matter what defects may exist within the framework of the United Nations, it still offers an alternate to a war of extinction.

Without the United Nations there would be chaos and doom; the physical being of the international body holds out the promise of a future world which will never know the abomination called war.

The League of Nations failed; the United Nations must not, for in its council chambers, ". . . we shall nobly save, or meanly lose, the last, best, hope of earth . . ." as Abraham Lincoln once said in another time of crisis and peril.

SUGGESTIONS FOR FURTHER READING

SUGGESTIONS
FOR FURTHER READING

The number of books on the First World War is enormous. Below I have listed a few which I believe will benefit any reader who desires to gain a wider knowledge of the terrible years, 1914-18, when the nations of the world engaged in the madness of what proved to be merely the first global war.

Falls, Cyril. *The Great War*. New York.: G. P. Putnam's Sons, 1959.

Graves, William S. *America's Siberian Adventure, 1918-1920*. New York: Jonathan Cape and Harrison Smith, 1931.

Halliday, E. M. *The Ignorant Armies*. New York: Harper and Brothers, 1958.

Jacobs, Bruce. *Heroes of the Army*. New York: W. W. Norton and Co., Inc. 1956.

Lawrence, Thomas E. *Revolt in the Desert*. New York: G. H. Doran Co., 1927.

Mitchell, William. *Memoirs of World War I*. New York: Random House, 1960.

Moorehead, Alan. *Gallipoli*. New York: Harper and Brothers, 1956.

O'Connor, Richard. *Black Jack Pershing*. New York: Doubleday and Co. Inc., 1961.

Oughton, Frederick. *The Aces*. New York: G. P. Putnam's Sons. 1960.

Pershing, John J. *My Experiences in the World War,* 2 vols. New York: Frederick A. Stokes Co., 1931.

Reiners, Ludwig. *The Lamps Went Out In Europe.* New York: Pantheon Books, Inc., 1955.

Remak, Joachim. *Sarajevo.* New York: Criterion Books, Inc., 1959.

Remarque, Erich Maria. *All Quiet on the Western Front.* Boston: Little, Brown & Co., 1929.

Reynolds, Quentin. *They Fought for the Sky.* New York: Rinehart & Co., 1957.

Seldes, George. *Sawdust Caesar.* New York: Harper and Brothers, 1935.

Sullivan, Mark. *Our Times: 1900-1925* (Vols. 4, 5). New York: Charles Scribner's Sons, 1936.

Tuchman, Barbara. *The Guns of August.* New York: The Macmillan Co., 1962.

Wolff, Leon. *In Flanders Fields.* New York: The Viking Press., 1958.

INDEX

INDEX

About the Author

IRVING WERSTEIN is a native-born New Yorker, still living in New York. He was born on May 22, 1914, graduated from Richmond Hill High School where he was on the staff of the school paper. He entered New York University in the early '30's to study advertising copy-writing, but family financial reverses necessitated his leaving after two years. He has been actor, waiter, camp counselor, factory worker, comedian, reporter. He sold his first short story in 1938, and except for a three-year stint in the Army, has made writing a full-time career. He has written radio and television scripts and is the author of both adult and juvenile books.